BEST PLACES NORTHWEST
COOKBOOK

2ND EDITION

CYNTHIA C. NIMS, LORI MCKEAN, AND LARA FERRONI

BEST PLACES NORTHWEST
COOKBOOK

**RECIPES FROM THE OUTSTANDING RESTAURANTS AND INNS
OF WASHINGTON, OREGON, AND BRITISH COLUMBIA**

SASQUATCH BOOKS
SEATTLE

Printed in Singapore by Star Standard Industries Pte Ltd.
Published by Sasquatch Books
Distributed by PGW/Perseus
15 14 13 12 11 10 09   9 8 7 6 5 4 3 2 1

Cover and interior design and composition: Kate Basart/Union Pageworks
Cover and interior photographs: Lara Ferroni
Text compiled by: Cynthia Nims, Lori McKean, and Lara Ferroni

Library of Congress Cataloging-in-Publication Data
Nims, Cynthia C.
Best places northwest cookbook : recipes from the outstanding restaurants and inns of Washington, Oregon,
and British Columbia / Cynthia Nims, Lori McKean & Lara Ferroni. -- 2nd ed.
p. cm.
Includes index.
ISBN-13: 978-1-57061-597-9
ISBN-10: 1-57061-597-7
1. Cookery, American--Pacific Northwest style. I. McKean, Lori. II. Ferroni, Lara. III. Title.
TX715.2.P32N56 2009
641.59795--dc22
2008050029

SASQUATCH BOOKS
119 South Main Street, Suite 400
Seattle, WA 98104
206/467-4300
www.sasquatchbooks.com
custserv@sasquatchbooks.com

contents

introduction

U pdating such a classic cookbook as The Northwest Best Places Cookbook was a challenge. Some of the contributing restaurants have closed shop or have gone through major changes and are no longer included in the Best Places guidebooks. Hundreds of new restaurants have sprouted up to take their places, bringing their own fresh interpretations to Northwest cuisine. How do you balance those classic recipes with new ones that represent the current tastes without losing something in the process?

In fact, the dining scene of the Pacific Northwest has grown up since the original publication of what was The Northwest Best Places Cookbook. The region has become a major influence in the culinary arts on a national level, bringing to light the importance of eating seasonally, organically, and locally. Oregon's organic certification program has set the new standard for what it means to be truly organic, and restaurants like Maria Hines' Tilth (only the second restaurant to achieve the certification in the country) rise to the occasion with dishes we all feel good about eating, not only because they are beneficial to the earth, but also because they are truly delicious. The 100-mile diet, started in Vancouver, British Columbia, has raised the level of discussion in the Northwest and around the country about what it means to eat locally. This new consciousness changed the way we think about where our food comes from and the personalities behind it.

Looking back though, the ideas that are now at the forefront of food politics still hold to the same principles that made Northwest cuisine something we've always celebrated: fresh, seasonal foods creatively prepared to a delectable end.

To create this second edition we've trimmed down a few of the recipes to best represent today's dining landscape and have added thirteen new recipes from some of the most highly regarded restaurants in the region. The collection is as diverse as ever, featuring the classic ingredients we've always known and loved, and pairing them with some new and unexpected items that are sure to surprise and delight.

—Lara Ferroni
May 2009

four seasons baked eggs

AMY'S MANOR BED & BREAKFAST ✦ PATEROS, WASHINGTON

The 170-acre estate at Amy's Manor includes a farm with chickens, rabbits, and an organic garden. Breakfasts at the inn always showcase farm-fresh ingredients, which, like this recipe, change with the seasons. Be sure to try your own adaptations, using seasonal vegetables and herbs from your garden or neighborhood market.

8 eggs
½ cup half-and-half
⅓ cup sour cream
¾ cup grated sharp cheddar cheese
Salt and freshly ground black pepper
1 tablespoon unsalted butter
Herb sprigs, for garnish

Spring
2 cups coarsely chopped arugula, spinach, and/or red mustard leaves
1 tablespoon minced chives

Summer
Kernels from 1 ear fresh sweet corn
8 large basil leaves, finely shredded
1 vine-ripe tomato, cut into ¼-inch slices

Fall
1 medium russet potato, scrubbed and cut into ½-inch dice
2 teaspoons fresh thyme leaves
½ teaspoon dried red pepper flakes

Winter
½ pound pork sausage
1 teaspoon dried sage leaves, crushed

PREHEAT THE OVEN to 350°F.

LIGHTLY WHISK TOGETHER the eggs, half-and-half, and sour cream. Stir in the cheese with a pinch each of salt and pepper. Place the butter in a heavy, ovenproof 10-inch skillet, preferably nonstick, and heat in the oven until melted, about 5 minutes.

Take the pan from the oven and swirl the butter evenly over the bottom of the pan. Add the egg mixture and bake until the eggs are just set but still moist, 20 to 25 minutes. Let cool for a few minutes, then slide the eggs onto a cutting board and cut into wedges. Arrange the wedges on a serving platter or individual plates, garnish with herb sprigs, and serve.

spring eggs

AFTER HEATING THE PAN with the butter, remove it from the oven and add the greens. Toss until wilted, then pour the egg mixture on top, sprinkle the chives over the eggs, and continue as directed in the base recipe.

summer eggs

AFTER HEATING THE PAN with the butter, remove it from the oven and add the corn. Toss until evenly coated in butter. Stir the basil into the egg mixture, then pour it into the pan. Continue as directed in the base recipe, arranging the tomato slices over the eggs after about 15 minutes of baking.

fall eggs

PLACE THE POTATO in a small pan of lightly salted water, bring to a boil, and cook until nearly tender, 5 to 7 minutes. Drain well.

AFTER HEATING THE PAN with the butter, remove it from the oven and add the diced potato. Toss until evenly coated in butter. Stir the thyme leaves and red pepper flakes into the egg mixture, then pour it into the pan. Continue as directed in the base recipe.

winter eggs

COOK THE SAUSAGE in a small skillet over medium heat, breaking it into small pieces, until no pink remains, about 10 minutes. Drain well, discarding the fat. Stir the sausage and sage into the egg mixture, pour it into the preheated pan, and continue as directed in the base recipe.

MAKES 6 SERVINGS

artichoke soufflés

THE BEACONSFIELD INN ◦ VICTORIA, BRITISH COLUMBIA

Soufflés have a reputation for being fussy and difficult to prepare. But not these. Baked in individual ½-cup ramekins, they puff to a golden brown when cooked. Made in larger portions, they would also make a delicious lunch.

6 eggs
¼ teaspoon hot pepper sauce
¼ cup flour
Pinch freshly ground nutmeg
1½ cups milk
1 can (14 ounces) artichoke hearts, drained and coarsely chopped
1 cup grated fontina cheese
1 cup grated cheddar cheese
½ cup chopped green onion or chives

PREHEAT THE OVEN to 350°F. Lightly grease eight ½-cup ramekins.

WHISK TOGETHER the eggs and hot pepper sauce in a large bowl until blended. Add the flour and nutmeg and mix well. Whisk in the milk, then stir in the artichoke hearts, cheeses, and green onion. Spoon the mixture into the ramekins, filling them to about ¼ inch below the rim. Set the ramekins on a baking sheet and bake until puffed and nicely browned, 45 to 50 minutes. Serve immediately.

MAKES 8 SERVINGS

dungeness crab quiche

GROVELAND COTTAGE ⟡ SEQUIM, WASHINGTON

Sweet, meaty Dungeness crab is the house specialty at this bed-and-breakfast located on Dungeness Way in Dungeness, a small fishing village on the Strait of Juan de Fuca. In addition to crab, this recipe calls for chanterelle mushrooms, but you can substitute common button mushrooms if wild mushrooms are not available.

½ pound chanterelles, cleaned, trimmed, and coarsely chopped
4 shallots, minced
1 tablespoon unsalted butter
1 tablespoon olive oil
2 tablespoons dried dill weed
1 tablespoon freshly squeezed lemon juice
Salt and hot pepper sauce or freshly ground black pepper
2 cups Dungeness crabmeat (about ¾ pound)
3 eggs
1 cup half-and-half
½ cup grated Parmesan cheese
2 tablespoons minced cilantro or flat-leaf (Italian) parsley, for garnish

Pastry Crust
1½ cups flour
6 tablespoons unsalted butter, cut into pieces
½ teaspoon salt
3 tablespoons chilled water (plus more if needed)

FOR THE CRUST, combine the flour, butter, and salt in a food processor (or with a pastry knife) and process until the mixture has the texture of coarse crumbs. Add the water and blend until the mixture just begins to form a ball, adding a little more water if needed. Turn the dough out onto a work surface, form it into a ball, and wrap it in plastic. Chill for at least 1 hour.

PREHEAT THE OVEN to 375°F.

ON A LIGHTLY FLOURED work surface, roll the dough into a circle about 14 inches in diameter. Line a 10-inch pie pan with the dough, trimming the excess as necessary and fluting the edges. Place a sheet of foil over the dough and cover the bottom with pie weights or dried beans. Bake the crust for 10 minutes; remove the foil and weights and continue baking until the crust is set and lightly browned, 18 to 20 minutes. Let cool.

REDUCE THE OVEN to 350°F.

HEAT A NONSTICK SKILLET over medium-high heat, add the mushrooms, and cook until they become tender and the liquid they release has evaporated, about 5 minutes. Add the shallots, butter, and oil and sauté until the shallots are tender but not browned, 2 to 3 minutes. Stir in the dill and lemon juice, adding salt and hot pepper sauce to taste. Take the skillet from the heat.

PICK OVER THE CRABMEAT to remove any bits of shell or cartilage. Add it to the skillet and stir until well mixed; set aside.

IN A MEDIUM BOWL, combine the eggs with the half-and-half and all but 2 tablespoons of the cheese.

SPREAD THE CRAB MIXTURE evenly in the pie shell. Pour the egg mixture over it and sprinkle the reserved 2 tablespoons of cheese over the top. Bake until a knife inserted into the quiche comes out clean, 35 to 40 minutes. Remove from the oven, sprinkle with the cilantro, and let sit 5 minutes before cutting to serve.

MAKES 8 SERVINGS

breakfast frittata

Guests who need to catch an early ferry often carry away this delicious frittata wrapped in a warm tortilla—hence its nickname, "ferry ta-ta." This recipe calls for turkey sausage, but any flavorful sausage can be substituted. For added zest, top the frittata with salsa.

> 2 tablespoons olive oil
> 6 ounces bulk sausage, preferably turkey
> 2 medium red potatoes, cut into ½-inch cubes
> 6 eggs
> 3 tablespoons water
> ½ teaspoon minced fresh dill or ¼ teaspoon dried dill weed
> ¼ teaspoon lemon pepper or freshly ground black pepper
> ⅛ teaspoon hot pepper sauce, plus more to taste
> Pinch salt
> 1 tablespoon unsalted butter
> ¼ cup diced green onion
> ¼ cup diced red bell pepper
> ½ cup grated cheddar cheese
> ¼ cup sour cream
> Herb sprigs and/or cherry tomatoes, for garnish

HEAT 1 TABLESPOON of the olive oil in a small skillet, add the sausage, and cook over medium heat, breaking the sausage into small pieces, until no pink remains, about 10 minutes. Drain well, discarding the fat.

BRING A SMALL PAN of water to a boil, add the diced potatoes, and boil for 5 minutes; drain well. In a medium bowl, combine the eggs, water, dill, pepper, hot pepper sauce, and salt.

HEAT THE REMAINING 1 tablespoon olive oil with the butter in a large skillet, preferably nonstick, over medium heat. Add the potatoes and fry until golden and crisp, about 10 minutes. Add the sausage, green onion, and bell pepper and cook for 1 minute longer.

POUR THE EGG MIXTURE over the vegetables and cook over medium heat, gently lifting the edges as the eggs set to help distribute the uncooked egg. Cook, covered, until the eggs are set and the bottom is lightly browned, 3 to 4 minutes.

SLIDE THE FRITTATA onto a serving platter, folding it in half. Sprinkle with the cheese and add a thick ribbon of sour cream. Garnish with herb sprigs and cherry tomatoes, and serve.

MAKES 4 SERVINGS

smoked salmon and chive potato pancakes

INN AT SWIFTS BAY ◆ LOPEZ ISLAND, WASHINGTON

Look for a firm, hot-smoked salmon to use in this recipe. A poached egg, cooked with Old Bay seasoning and vinegar, is a great addition served alongside these hearty pancakes. Note that the cottage cheese and ricotta topping must be prepared the night before.

Topping

1 cup nonfat cottage cheese

¼ cup nonfat, low-salt ricotta cheese

1 teaspoon freshly squeezed lemon juice, plus more to taste

Pancakes

3 pounds white or russet potatoes

3 eggs, lightly beaten

½ cup chopped chives, plus more for garnish

½ cup finely chopped onion

⅓ cup all-purpose flour or potato flour

2 teaspoons no-salt seafood seasoning mix, such as MarketSpice brand

1 teaspoon Old Bay seasoning

½ teaspoon baking powder

¼ teaspoon freshly ground black pepper

6 to 8 ounces hot-smoked salmon, skin and bones removed, finely chopped

1 to 2 tablespoons olive oil

Freshly grated lemon zest, for garnish

PREPARE THE TOPPING the night before serving. Combine the cottage cheese and ricotta in a colander and let sit for at least 1 hour to drain slightly. Place the cheese mixture in a food processor with the lemon juice and process until very smooth, about 3 minutes. Taste for tartness, adding more lemon juice to taste. Transfer to a bowl, cover, and refrigerate overnight to thicken.

FOR THE PANCAKES, peel the potatoes and grate them. Rinse them in a colander in cold water (or in Fruit-Fresh—a commercial antioxidant that will prevent them from graying), then wrap them in a dish towel and squeeze to remove all excess moisture. In a large bowl, combine the eggs, chives, onion, flour, seafood seasoning, Old Bay seasoning, baking powder, and pepper. Stir in the salmon and potatoes. Line a baking sheet with cut-up brown paper bags for holding the cooked pancakes.

HEAT A LARGE FRYING PAN, preferably nonstick, with some of the olive oil. Stir the potato mixture again and scoop a few pancakes into the pan, using about ¼ cup batter for each pancake. Flatten them with a spatula. Cook until nicely browned, about 2 to 3 minutes on each side. Transfer the pancakes to the paper-lined baking sheet and keep warm in a low oven. Continue with the remaining potato mixture.

TO SERVE, arrange 3 potato pancakes on each individual warmed plate. Scoop a generous spoonful of the topping over the pancakes and sprinkle with chopped chives and lemon zest.

MAKES 6 SERVINGS

brioche french toast with caramelized pineapple

MONSOON • SEATTLE, WASHINGTON

Rich slices of brioche almost turn this delectable dish into a pudding. If you can't find brioche (and don't feel like making your own), challah bread or even thick slices of French bread will work just as well.

¾ cup brown sugar

8 rings of fresh pineapple, about ½ inch thick

3 large eggs

2 cups half-and-half

2 tablespoons five-spice powder

2 tablespoons vanilla extract

Brioche loaf, cut into four 1-inch-thick slices

3 tablespoons unsalted butter, preferably clarified butter

Powdered sugar

TO CARAMELIZE THE PINEAPPLE, spread the brown sugar on a salad plate. Place pineapple slices, one at a time, in the brown sugar and turn to coat both sides with a thin layer of the sugar. Set aside.

HEAT A NONSTICK SAUTÉ PAN large enough to accommodate four slices of pineapple (or cook in batches) over medium heat. Cook the pineapple slices until browned, 2 to 3 minutes on each side. Repeat with the remaining pineapple rings. Set aside.

TO MAKE THE FRENCH TOAST, in a flat baking dish big enough to hold at least 2 slices of brioche, combine the eggs, half-and-half, five-spice powder, and vanilla. Soak the brioche slices in the custard until soaked through, about 1 minute on each side.

MEANWHILE, in a large sauté pan, melt 1½ tablespoons of the butter over medium heat. Using a spatula, transfer the soaked brioche slices to the pan. Fry on both sides until golden brown, 2 to 3 minutes on each side. Repeat with the remaining slices of brioche, adding more butter as needed.

TO SERVE, cut each piece of toast in half. Place 2 halves on each serving plate. Dust with powdered sugar and serve with the caramelized pineapple on the side.

MAKES 4 SERVINGS

mount adams huckleberry hotcakes

THE FLYING L RANCH • GLENWOOD, WASHINGTON

Forty years ago, Ilse Lloyd presided over the stove at The Flying L Ranch. Today, the new owners, Julee Wasserman and Tim Johnson, still flip out the ranch's favorite hotcakes bubbling with berries picked from the nearby huckleberry fields.

> 3 cups flour
> ¾ cup rolled oats
> ¼ cup oat bran or 100-percent bran cereal
> 4 teaspoons baking powder
> 2 teaspoons baking soda
> ½ teaspoon salt (optional)
> 4 eggs
> 4 cups buttermilk, plus more if needed
> ¼ cup vegetable oil
> 1 to 2 cups huckleberries, fresh or frozen (blueberries make a good
>   substitute if huckleberries aren't available)

STIR TOGETHER the flour, oats, oat bran, baking powder, baking soda, and salt in a large bowl. In another bowl, beat the eggs, then stir in the buttermilk and oil. Add the egg mixture to the flour mixture and stir gently until just blended. If the batter is too thick, stir in a little more buttermilk.

HEAT A GRIDDLE or a large, heavy skillet, preferably nonstick (if not nonstick, brush lightly with oil). Stir the huckleberries into the batter. Pour ¼ cup batter onto the griddle for each pancake. Cook until bubbly on top, then flip and continue cooking until nicely browned, 2 to 3 minutes on each side. Serve with your favorite syrup or fresh fruit jam.

MAKES 6 TO 8 SERVINGS

berry sense

Plump, juicy, and fresh from the bush or vine, berries are some of nature's sweetest, healthiest, and most delicious foods. Berries are low in calories, averaging about 80 per cup, and are packed with vitamins, potassium, iron, and calcium. Fresh berries are also an excellent source of natural fiber and one of the top disease-fighting, antioxidant foods around.

When selecting berries, choose firm, plump fruit that is brightly colored and full flavored. Berries will keep for several days in the refrigerator but are best when freshly picked. Don't wash berries until it's time to use them. Wash gently and thoroughly under cold water and drain on paper towels. To prevent strawberries from absorbing water, don't hull them until they have been washed and dried. Raspberries and other hollow berries often benefit from being dropped gently on a towel to release any bugs that may be hiding inside.

Caneberries—including blackberries, raspberries, salmonberries, and so on—freeze well: Simply wash the berries, then lay them in a single layer on a tray or cookie sheet. Freeze until firm, then pack the berries into freezer bags or containers and return to the freezer. They will keep for up to nine months.

elvis pancakes

RAM'S HEAD INN ❖ ROSSLAND, BRITISH COLUMBIA

Elvis loved grilled peanut butter and banana sandwiches. But unless you've stayed at the Ram's Head Inn—a mountain resort in Rossland, British Columbia—you probably don't know about The King's other favorite: peanut butter and banana pancakes topped with real maple syrup and butter. Local legend has it that Elvis insists on these pancakes every time he comes to ski at Red Mountain.

> 2 eggs
> 2 cups buttermilk
> 1 cup chunky peanut butter
> ¼ cup vegetable oil
> 1½ cups flour, plus more if needed
> 2 tablespoons sugar
> 1 teaspoon baking powder
> ½ teaspoon salt
> 2 or 3 ripe bananas, peeled and cut into ¼-inch slices

LIGHTLY BEAT THE EGGS in a large bowl, then add the buttermilk, peanut butter, and oil and whisk until well mixed. Sift together the flour, sugar, baking powder, and salt and add to the egg mixture. Stir gently just until blended, adding a little more flour only if the batter is too thin; it should still have a few lumps.

HEAT A GRIDDLE or large, heavy skillet and oil it lightly. Pour the batter onto the griddle, using about ⅓ cup for each pancake, and cook over moderate heat until the edges look dry and bubbles appear on top, 2 to 3 minutes. Arrange about 4 slices of banana on top of each pancake, then turn and continue cooking until browned on the other side, about 2 minutes longer. Serve banana side up, with maple syrup and butter if you like.

MAKES 4 TO 6 SERVINGS

mary's oatmeal pancakes

SALISBURY HOUSE ◆ SEATTLE, WASHINGTON

For these surprisingly light and fluffy pancakes, the oats soak in buttermilk overnight; they add body, texture, and a certain richness to the batter without weighing it down. Top the pancakes off with real maple syrup and sour cream or yogurt.

2 cups rolled oats
3 cups buttermilk
½ cup flour
1 teaspoon baking soda
1 teaspoon baking powder
¼ teaspoon salt
2 eggs, lightly beaten
¼ cup vegetable oil

Chunky Applesauce
3 Golden Delicious apples, peeled, cored, and sliced
⅓ cup water
¼ cup granulated sugar, plus more to taste
½ teaspoon ground cinnamon, plus more to taste

THE NIGHT BEFORE making the pancakes, combine the oats and buttermilk in a large bowl, stir to mix, cover, and refrigerate overnight.

FOR THE APPLESAUCE, combine the apples with the water in a medium saucepan and cook over low heat until the apples are soft but still holding together, 12 to 15 minutes. Stir in sugar and cinnamon to taste; set aside.

JUST BEFORE SERVING, combine the flour, baking soda, baking powder, and salt in a large bowl. In another bowl, stir together the eggs and vegetable oil. Add the egg mixture to the flour mixture, followed by the oatmeal mixture. Stir gently to mix well. Pour about ¼ cup of batter onto a lightly oiled hot griddle and cook until golden brown, about 2 minutes on each side. Serve hot, with the applesauce on the side.

MAKES 4 TO 6 SERVINGS

kaiserschmarren
(austrian pancake)

DURLACHER HOF ✦ WHISTLER, BRITISH COLUMBIA

In the ski country of Austria, Kaiserschmarren *is served not only for breakfast but also for afternoon dessert with plenty of good, strong coffee. Legend has it that Austrian Emperor Franz Josef always tore his pancakes into small bits before eating them, and that's how they're served at the Durlacher Hof, lightly dusted with powdered sugar. Stewed prunes or cherries are a good accompaniment (or try the Winter Fruit Compote on page 23).*

> 2 cups flour
> 1 cup milk
> ½ cup unsalted butter
> Pinch salt
> 4 eggs, separated
> ¼ cup sugar
> ½ cup raisins
> Fresh or stewed fruit, for serving
> Powdered sugar, for sprinkling

PREHEAT THE OVEN to 375°F.

STIR TOGETHER the flour and milk in a large bowl. Melt ¼ cup of the butter and whisk it into the batter with the salt, then whisk in the egg yolks.

BEAT THE EGG WHITES with the sugar in a separate bowl until firm and glossy, then gently fold them into the batter.

HEAT THE REMAINING ¼ cup butter in a 12-inch cast iron skillet. Carefully pour in the batter and scatter the raisins evenly over it. Bake the pancake in the preheated oven until puffed and golden, 20 to 25 minutes. Using two forks, tear the pancake into serving pieces and arrange on individual plates. Spoon some fruit onto the pancake and sprinkle powdered sugar over it. Serve immediately.

MAKES 8 TO 10 SERVINGS

harvest muffins

Innkeeper Peter Goldfarb serves these fragrant muffins hot from the oven, accompanied by fresh fruit from his orchard and dark-roast coffee. The secret to baking great muffins is to stir the batter gently, just until ingredients are blended. Don't worry if the batter is still a bit lumpy; overmixing will prevent it from rising properly.

2 cups flour
½ cup rolled oats
1 tablespoon ground cinnamon
2 teaspoons baking powder
1 teaspoon baking soda
1 teaspoon ground ginger
1 teaspoon salt
1 cup milk
1 carrot, grated (about 1 cup)
½ cup packed brown sugar
½ cup raisins
½ cup fresh cranberries, coarsely chopped
½ cup vegetable oil
1 egg
2 tablespoons molasses

PREHEAT THE OVEN to 400°F. Lightly grease a 12-cup muffin tin.

COMBINE THE FLOUR, oats, cinnamon, baking powder, baking soda, ginger, and salt in a large bowl. In another bowl, stir together the milk, carrot, brown sugar, raisins, cranberries, oil, egg, and molasses.

ADD THE WET INGREDIENTS to the dry ingredients, stirring gently until just blended but still a little lumpy. Pour the batter into the muffin tins, filling each to just below the rim. Bake until a toothpick inserted in the center of a muffin comes out clean, 15 to 18 minutes.

MAKES 12 MUFFINS

gingerbread crepes with apple filling

QUIMPER INN ❦ PORT TOWNSEND, WASHINGTON

This fall recipe is good any time of year. You'll need only eight crepes for this recipe, so don't worry if the first few don't work out. Extra crepes can be wrapped in plastic wrap and foil and frozen for later use. Tart, firm apples, such as Gravensteins or Granny Smiths, work best.

Crepes

1 cup flour

1 to 2 tablespoons sugar

1 teaspoon ground ginger

1 teaspoon ground cinnamon

Pinch ground cloves

1⅓ cups milk

2 eggs

¼ cup molasses

1 tablespoon unsalted butter, melted, plus more for cooking the crepes

Apple Filling

¼ cup unsalted butter

3 large, firm apples, peeled, cored, and sliced

½ cup hot water, plus more if needed

¼ cup sugar

1 tablespoon ground cinnamon, plus more to taste

✄

Unsweetened whipped cream, for serving

Chopped walnuts, for serving

FOR THE CREPES, combine the flour, sugar, ginger, cinnamon, and cloves in a large bowl. In another bowl, combine the milk, eggs, molasses, and melted butter. Make a shallow well in the center of the dry mixture, add the wet mixture, and stir gently just until well combined.

HEAT ABOUT 2 TEASPOONS of butter in a crepe pan or small skillet, preferably nonstick, over medium heat. Add about ¼ cup of the crepe batter, tilting the pan so it evenly covers the bottom. Cook until the top is set and the edges begin to brown, 1 to 2 minutes. Turn the crepe and continue cooking just until the other side is lightly browned, about 1 minute longer. Turn the crepe onto a plate and continue with the remaining batter, adding more butter as necessary. Put a piece of waxed paper or plastic wrap over each crepe to make them easier to separate later. The crepes can be made a day in advance and refrigerated, covered.

FOR THE APPLE FILLING, melt the butter in a large skillet, add the apple slices, and cook, stirring, until they are well coated in butter, 1 to 2 minutes. Add the water, sugar, and cinnamon and continue cooking, uncovered, until the apples are tender but not mushy, 12 to 15 minutes longer. The sauce should be syrupy; add a little more water if needed.

TO ASSEMBLE THE CREPES, reheat them, if necessary, in the oven on low heat. Place some of the apple slices down the center of each crepe and roll it up. Arrange 2 filled crepes on each plate and drizzle with a little of the sauce from the apples. Top the crepes with a dollop of whipped cream and a sprinkle of chopped walnuts. Serve immediately.

MAKES 4 SERVINGS

winter fruit compote

ABIGAIL'S HOTEL ✦ VICTORIA, BRITISH COLUMBIA

Sprinkled with toasted walnuts, this elegant fruit compote is great for breakfast or dessert. The recipe calls for Sauternes, a dessert wine produced in France; however, any of the numerous fine dessert wines from the Northwest will work equally well. Look for "late harvest" wines that have been affected by Botrytis cinerea, "the noble rot."

¾ cup sugar

½ cup water

½ cup Sauternes or other dessert wine

4 cinnamon sticks

¼ cup freshly squeezed lemon juice

4 Granny Smith apples, peeled, cored, and cut into 1-inch chunks

1 cup cranberries (fresh or frozen)

4 pears, preferably Bosc, peeled, cored, and cut into 1-inch chunks

½ cup walnuts, toasted and chopped into large pieces

COMBINE THE SUGAR, water, Sauternes, cinnamon sticks, and lemon juice in a large, heavy saucepan. Bring to a boil, stirring often, and boil until reduced by about one third, 8 to 10 minutes. Add the apples and cook over medium heat, stirring occasionally, until just tender, 5 to 6 minutes. Stir in the cranberries and cook for a few minutes longer. Remove the pan from the heat, stir in the pears, and let sit for a few minutes until the liquid has cooled slightly. Discard the cinnamon sticks and spoon the fruit and sauce into individual bowls. Sprinkle the walnuts over the compote and serve.

MAKES 4 TO 6 SERVINGS

wild blackberry coffee cake

EAGLES NEST INN ❖ LANGLEY, WASHINGTON

Packed with plump, juicy blackberries, this coffee cake is a favorite during the summer months at the Eagles Nest Inn, where blackberries abound. Frozen blackberries can be substituted for fresh; however, if you use frozen berries, plan to bake the cake for an extra 20 minutes. What you don't finish in the morning will keep well for an afternoon snack or evening dessert, even a day or two later.

Coffee cake

⅓ cup packed brown sugar

⅓ cup chopped walnuts

2½ cups flour

½ cup granulated sugar

2 teaspoons baking powder

¼ teaspoon salt

1 cup milk

¼ cup unsalted butter, melted and cooled slightly

1 egg

½ teaspoon almond extract or vanilla extract

¼ teaspoon freshly ground nutmeg

⅓ cup shredded coconut

2 cups fresh wild blackberries or frozen whole blackberries (do not thaw if frozen)

Glaze

½ cup powdered sugar

2 teaspoons milk

PREHEAT THE OVEN to 375°F. Lightly grease the bottom and sides of a 9-inch round, deep baking dish such as a quiche dish.

STIR TOGETHER the brown sugar and walnuts in a small bowl; set aside.

SIFT THE FLOUR. Combine the flour, granulated sugar, baking powder, and salt in a large bowl. Whisk in the milk, melted butter, egg, almond extract, and nutmeg until smooth and well mixed. Spread about two-thirds of the batter in the prepared pan. Sprinkle the coconut evenly over it. Scatter half of the blackberries over the batter, pushing them slightly into it.

SPOON THE REMAINING BATTER into the dish, gently spreading it toward the edges; you don't need to cover the berries completely. Scatter the remaining berries over the top. Sprinkle the brown sugar and walnuts evenly over the berries. Bake until a toothpick inserted in the center comes out clean, 40 to 45 minutes. Let cool.

FOR THE GLAZE, combine the powdered sugar and milk in a small bowl and stir until the sugar dissolves. Drizzle the glaze over the coffee cake, beginning in the center and working in a spiral toward the outer edge. Cut into wedges and serve.

MAKES 8 SERVINGS

cinnamon buns

THE OLD FARMHOUSE ◦ SALT SPRING ISLAND, BRITISH COLUMBIA

These power breakfast rolls receive raves from the guests at this three-star island inn. Giant-size, they're enhanced with fruits and spices that will arouse your morning taste buds.

1 small navel orange
⅓ cup warm water
2 tablespoons (2 packages) active dry yeast
½ cup plus 1 tablespoon granulated sugar
¾ cup milk
½ cup unsalted butter
⅓ cup buttermilk
¼ cup sour cream
6 cups flour, plus more if needed
2 eggs
1 teaspoon salt

Filling
½ cup unsalted butter, softened
¾ cup packed brown sugar
¾ cup raisins
2 tablespoons ground cinnamon
2 small apples, peeled, cored, and thinly sliced

Glaze
½ cup powdered sugar
2 tablespoons freshly squeezed orange juice

WASH THE RIND of the orange and cut it into quarters. Purée the entire orange in a food processor until smooth. Set aside.

STIR TOGETHER the warm water, yeast, and 1 tablespoon of the sugar in a small bowl. Let sit until frothy, 8 to 10 minutes.

COMBINE THE MILK, butter, buttermilk, and sour cream in a medium saucepan and warm over low heat until the butter is melted. Set aside to cool until the mixture is lukewarm.

COMBINE 1 CUP of the flour with the remaining ½ cup sugar, eggs, puréed orange, salt, and the warm milk mixture in the large bowl of an electric mixer fitted with a paddle attachment, or by hand with a wooden spoon. Beat thoroughly. Add the yeast mixture and beat for 2 to 3 minutes longer. Add another cup of flour and continue beating for another minute.

ADD THE REMAINING FLOUR, ½ cup at a time, beating until the dough is smooth and supple. (When the dough begins to form a ball, change to the dough hook attachment if your machine has one, or start to gently knead the dough with lightly floured hands on a floured work surface.) Avoid adding too much flour; it's better the dough be a little sticky than too dry. Cover the bowl with a damp cloth and let rise in a warm place until doubled in bulk, about 1 hour.

PUNCH DOWN THE DOUGH, turn it out onto a lightly floured work surface, and roll it out into a rectangle about ½ inch thick (roughly 16 inches by 20 inches). Spread the softened butter over the dough and sprinkle evenly with the brown sugar, raisins, and cinnamon. Arrange the apple slices in lengthwise rows over the filling. Roll the dough up into a cylinder and cut it into 12 slices, each about 1½ inches thick. Arrange the slices on two lightly greased baking sheets, at least 1 inch apart. Cover with a cloth and let rise until doubled, 45 minutes to 1 hour.

PREHEAT THE OVEN to 350°F.

BAKE THE CINNAMON BUNS until nicely browned and puffed, 8 to 12 minutes. Meanwhile, stir together the powdered sugar and orange juice for the glaze. When the cinnamon buns come from the oven, drizzle the glaze over them and let cool slightly in the pan. Serve warm.

MAKES 12 BUNS

lemon cheese braid

ROMEO INN   ·   ASHLAND, OREGON

Innkeepers Don and Deana Politis try to keep things fresh at the Romeo Inn so you rarely get the same breakfast twice. The problem is, once you've tasted their zesty raisin-and cream cheese–filled bread, you will want to eat it again.

1 tablespoon (1 package) active dry yeast

¼ cup warm water

3 to 4 cups flour

½ cup milk, scalded and slightly cooled

2 eggs

¼ cup granulated sugar

¼ cup unsalted butter, softened

½ teaspoon salt

Filling

12 ounces cream cheese, softened

½ cup granulated sugar

1 egg

1 teaspoon grated lemon zest

½ cup raisins

Icing

½ cup powdered sugar

2 tablespoons freshly squeezed lemon juice

1 tablespoon unsalted butter, melted

STIR THE YEAST into the warm water in a small bowl and let sit until frothy, 3 to 4 minutes.

IN A LARGE BOWL, combine 2 cups of the flour with the yeast mixture, milk, eggs, sugar, butter, and salt and mix well with an electric mixer fitted with a dough hook attachment or with a wooden spoon. Add enough of the remaining flour, ¼ cup at a time, to form a soft dough. Knead the dough until very smooth and elastic, 5 to 10 minutes. Place the dough in a greased bowl, cover, and let rise in a warm place until doubled in bulk, about 1 hour.

PREPARE THE FILLING while the dough is rising. Using an electric mixer or a large whisk, beat the cream cheese until smooth, gradually adding the sugar. Add the egg and lemon zest and continue beating until well mixed. Stir in the raisins and set aside.

PUNCH DOWN THE DOUGH, turn it out onto a lightly floured work surface, and roll it out into a rectangle about 12 inches by 14 inches. Transfer the dough to a lightly greased baking sheet. Spread the filling lengthwise down the center third of the dough. Using a small, sharp knife or kitchen shears, cut the uncovered outer thirds of the dough in 1-inch strips from the outer edge toward the filling. Beginning at one end, fold the strips over the filling, alternating from side to side, creating a braided effect. Cover and let rise again until doubled in bulk, about 45 minutes.

PREHEAT THE OVEN to 375°F.

BAKE THE BRAID until nicely browned, about 25 minutes. Transfer it to a wire rack to cool.

FOR THE ICING, stir together the powdered sugar, lemon juice, and melted butter until smooth; drizzle over the cooled braid. Cut into slices and serve.

MAKES 1 LARGE LOAF, 8 TO 12 SERVINGS

appetizers

pepper-cured smoked salmon

STONEHEDGE GARDENS ❉ HOOD RIVER, OREGON

This spicy smoked salmon is marinated in a fragrant brine flavored with garlic, white wine, juniper berries, cardamom, and black pepper, then delicately smoked over hardwood. The chefs at Stonehedge Gardens swear by their Luhr Jensen Little Chief Smoker, but you can use an electric or charcoal smoker. The sauce verte is best made at least a few hours in advance.

2 cups warm water

1½ cups white wine

1 cup packed light brown sugar

½ cup kosher salt

1 tablespoon chopped garlic

1 tablespoon whole green cardamom pods, lightly crushed

1 tablespoon juniper berries, lightly crushed

1 teaspoon thyme leaves

2 to 3 pounds salmon fillets, skin and bones removed

3 to 4 tablespoons cracked black peppercorns

Sauce Verte

2 cups mayonnaise

3 tablespoons minced cilantro

3 tablespoons minced flat-leaf (Italian) parsley

2 tablespoons honey

2 tablespoons stone-ground mustard

1 tablespoon minced chives

1 tablespoon minced tarragon

1 clove garlic, minced

Splash of freshly squeezed lemon juice

FOR THE LITTLE CHIEF SMOKER, very fine chips of wood (alder is a favorite) are used dry, and the electric heat source maintains a very low temperature, so 2 to 3 hours may be needed to smoke a fillet of fish (and chips may need replenishing during that time). For charcoal-heated smokers, larger chunks of wood chips are used and they are usually soaked in water before adding to the coals, so the chips produce more smoke for a longer time. Depending on the heat of the charcoal smoker, the fish can be smoked in 1 to 2 hours.

COMBINE THE WARM WATER, wine, brown sugar, salt, garlic, cardamom, juniper, and thyme in a 9- by 13-inch baking dish and stir until the sugar and salt have dissolved. Let cool completely.

CUT THE SALMON into 4-ounce pieces and set them in the brine. Let cure in the refrigerator for 6 to 8 hours.

FOR THE SAUCE VERTE, combine the mayonnaise, cilantro, parsley, honey, mustard, chives, tarragon, garlic, and lemon juice and whisk to mix well. Refrigerate until needed.

PREHEAT THE SMOKER according to the manufacturer's directions; if necessary, soak the smoking chips.

REMOVE THE SALMON from the brine, discarding the brine. Rinse the fish and dry it well with paper towels. Sprinkle the salmon pieces liberally with the cracked black peppercorns, pressing the peppercorns gently to help them adhere to the fish. Arrange the salmon on the racks in the smoker and gently smoke for 1 to 3 hours, depending on the type of smoker used. When finished, the salmon will form a skin and will lightly crack when pressed with a finger, but will still be tender and moist at the center.

LET THE SALMON COOL and serve it with the sauce verte on the side.

MAKES 8 TO 12 SERVINGS

warm salmon spread

MOUNT ASHLAND INN ✦ ASHLAND, OREGON

At the Mount Ashland Inn they use jars of home-smoked salmon in this horseradish-spiked spread. Use your favorite hot-smoked salmon for this easy-to-prepare appetizer. Serve with breads and crackers or with fresh vegetables.

8 ounces hot-smoked salmon, skin and bones removed
8 ounces cream cheese, softened
2 tablespoons minced sweet onion
1 tablespoon milk
1 tablespoon prepared horseradish
Salt and freshly ground black pepper
⅓ cup slivered almonds

PREHEAT THE OVEN to 375°F.

STIR TOGETHER the smoked salmon, cream cheese, onion, milk, and horseradish in a medium bowl. Add salt and pepper to taste. When well blended, put the mixture in a small baking dish, preferably one suitable for serving. Sprinkle the almonds on top and bake until the mixture is bubbly and the almonds are lightly browned, 12 to 15 minutes. Serve warm.

MAKES 4 TO 6 SERVINGS

smoked seafood

When buying smoked fish, look for flesh that glows, like fresh fish. It should smell sweet and clean like the sea, with a subtle balance of natural alder (or other hardwood) smoke flavor. Avoid smoked salmon that has been dyed red, fish that lists liquid smoke as an ingredient, or any fish that smells "fishy."

HOT-SMOKED: Seafood that has been cooked, after being smoked, to an internal temperature of 145°F. The seafood is first cured in salt or brine; then it is drained, dried, smoked, cooked, and cooled. Hot-smoked salmon is moist, firm, and meaty, with the buttery texture and earthy sweetness prized by salmon connoisseurs. When recipes call for smoked salmon as an ingredient, hot-smoked salmon is preferred.

COLD-SMOKED: Seafood that has been smoked but not cooked, with internal temperatures reaching no higher than 85°F. In the cold-smoking process, seafood is first dry-cured; then it is smoked and cooled. Silky and tender, slices of cold-smoked seafood melt on the palate with a velvety softness and a buttery finish. Cold-smoked salmon, and salmon cured by other means (such as those listed below), are best enjoyed as is.

NOVA: The term "Nova" refers to Nova Scotia, where many New York fish smokers used to buy their salmon. This cold-smoked salmon is typically less salty than lox.

LOX: Salmon that has been cured in a salty brine for up to a year and sometimes, but rarely, lightly smoked.

KIPPERED: Traditionally a British product, kippers are cold-smoked, split fat herring. In the United States, "kippered" (also known as "Northwest-style") usually refers to hot-smoked seafood with a high moisture content.

GRAVLAX: Uncooked salmon that has been cured in a mixture of salt, sugar, pepper, dill, and sometimes distilled spirits (not smoked). In Scandinavia, gravlax was traditionally buried in the earth to cure (sometimes for over a year), hence the name grav, meaning "grave."

DRIED (JERKY): Sometimes called "Indian hard-cure salmon," this is salmon that has been cured and then dried (sometimes by smoking).

dungeness crab wontons with thai dipping sauce

THE BAY HOUSE ◆ LINCOLN CITY, OREGON

Filled with sweet Dungeness crab and minced vegetables, these fragrant wontons are dipped in a spicy sauce flavored with hot chile oil and Thai fish sauce. If you can't find Thai fish sauce in the specialty food section of your local market, soy sauce can be substituted. Wonton skins are available in the produce section of many supermarkets. When making the wontons, be sure to squeeze excess liquid from the crab and chopped vegetable mixture. For a change of pace, you can pan-fry the wontons rather than simmering them. Pair them with a crisp, spicy Oregon pinot gris.

Wontons

4 ounces Dungeness crabmeat

½ cup chopped napa cabbage

¼ cup chopped bok choy

2 tablespoons grated carrot

1 tablespoon minced green onion

1 tablespoon minced red bell pepper

1 tablespoon minced green bell pepper

1 tablespoon minced ginger

1 tablespoon minced cilantro

16 wonton skins

1 egg

2 tablespoons cold water

Black sesame seeds, for garnish (optional)

Cilantro sprigs, for garnish

Thai Dipping Sauce

½ cup seasoned rice wine vinegar

1½ teaspoons Thai fish sauce (*nam pla*)

1½ teaspoons hot chile oil

FOR THE FILLING, pick over the crabmeat to remove any bits of shell or cartilage, then squeeze the crabmeat to remove excess moisture. Combine the cabbage, bok choy, carrot, green onion, red and green peppers, ginger, and cilantro in a food processor and pulse to finely chop and thoroughly mix, 3 to 4 pulses. Alternatively, chop each of the vegetables finely and mix well. Squeeze the chopped vegetables to remove excess moisture. Put the vegetables in a bowl with the crab and toss to mix well.

FOR THE THAI DIPPING SAUCE, stir together the vinegar and fish sauce in a small bowl. Add the hot chile oil to taste and set aside.

LAY THE WONTON SKINS on a lightly floured work surface. Whisk together the egg and water in a small bowl. Put a scant tablespoon of the crab filling in the center of each wonton skin. Lightly brush the edges with the egg mixture and fold the edges over to form triangles, pressing the edges well to seal.

BRING A LARGE PAN of water to a boil and lower the heat to a simmer. Add the wontons, a few at a time, and cook in the simmering water until just tender, 2 to 3 minutes. Scoop them out with a slotted spoon and drain well. Arrange the drained wontons on a serving platter with a small bowl of Thai dipping sauce. Sprinkle the black sesame seeds over them, garnish with sprigs of cilantro, and serve immediately.

MAKES 4 SERVINGS

polenta-encrusted crab with wild mushroom tapenade

THE BAY CAFÉ ✤ LOPEZ ISLAND, WASHINGTON

Filled with sweet Dungeness crab, these savory polenta "muffins" are topped with a wild mushroom tapenade. Match this appetizer with a rich, dry riesling. Both the polenta and the tapenade can be made a day in advance.

Mushroom Tapenade

2 tablespoons olive oil

6 ounces wild mushrooms (boletus, chanterelle, oyster, and/or shiitake mushrooms), cleaned, trimmed, and sliced

2 cloves garlic, minced

½ cup chicken stock (see page 108)

¼ cup minced flat-leaf (Italian) parsley

3 tablespoons chopped sun-dried tomatoes (oil-packed)

2 tablespoons capers

1 tablespoon freshly squeezed lemon juice

✖

½ pound Dungeness crabmeat

2 cups milk

2 cups water

1 cup polenta-grind (coarse) cornmeal

½ cup grated Parmesan cheese

½ cup grated Swiss cheese

Salt and freshly ground black pepper

FOR THE TAPENADE, heat the olive oil in a medium-size skillet, add the mushrooms and garlic, and sauté for 2 minutes over medium-high heat. Add the chicken stock, reduce the heat, and simmer until the mushrooms are very tender and most of the liquid has been absorbed, 15 to 20 minutes. Transfer the mixture to a bowl, add the parsley, sun-dried tomatoes, capers, and lemon juice, and toss to mix well. Set aside or refrigerate for up to a day.

REMOVE ANY BITS OF SHELL or cartilage from the crabmeat.

COMBINE THE MILK, water, and cornmeal in a medium-sized, heavy saucepan and bring to a boil, whisking constantly. Reduce the heat to medium and continue cooking for 20 minutes, whisking often. Remove the pan from the heat and stir in the Parmesan and Swiss cheeses, adding salt and pepper to taste.

LIGHTLY GREASE a 12-cup muffin tin. Half-fill each of the cups with the warm polenta mixture. Divide the crabmeat evenly among the muffin cups, pressing it gently into the polenta. Top the crab with the remaining polenta and use your fingers, moistened with water, to smooth the tops. Refrigerate until thoroughly chilled, at least 30 minutes and up to a day.

PREHEAT THE OVEN to 350°F.

UNMOLD THE POLENTAS upside-down onto a lightly greased baking sheet and bake until very hot and lightly browned, 25 to 30 minutes. Set one polenta on each plate, topped with some of the mushroom tapenade, and serve.

MAKES 12 SERVINGS

matching northwest wines and foods

Outstanding food and wine matches usually involve a combination of contrasts and similarities. Here in the Pacific Northwest, certain pairings of regional foods and wines are quickly becoming classics. Magic happens when you combine an earthy pinot noir, packed with flavors of fresh berries and spice, with the buttery-rich flavor of salmon. Another popular combination is cracked Dungeness crab and dry riesling; the crab is superbly matched by the wine's crisp, refreshing fruit and tangy mineral flavors.

By experimenting, you can invent a classic pairing of your own. Match a rich, velvety merlot with tender Northwest lamb. Enjoy a crisp, herbaceous semillon with local goat cheese. Pair pinot gris with mussels and vegetarian dishes. Or serve nectar-sweet late-harvest wines with Oregon blue cheese, toasted hazelnuts, and apple desserts.

spicy singapore prawns

KASTEEL FRANSSEN ◆ OAK HARBOR, WASHINGTON

Served on a bed of sweet-and-sour bean thread noodles, these fragrant prawns are spiced with hot red pepper flakes, garlic, and cilantro. The heat of this dish calls for a spicy Northwest riesling with a hint of sweetness, such as a Paul Thomas dry riesling.

1 package (3½ ounces) bean thread noodles
1¼ cups rice wine vinegar
1 cup sugar
1 cup water
1 tablespoon peanut or vegetable oil
20 large shrimp (about 1 pound), peeled and deveined
2 tablespoons minced garlic
2 tablespoons chopped green onion
1 tablespoon chopped cilantro
2 to 3 teaspoons dried red pepper flakes
¼ cup white wine
1 tablespoon soy sauce
½ cup unsalted butter, cut into pieces and chilled

BRING A LARGE PAN of water to a boil, add the bean thread noodles, and cook until tender, about 5 minutes. Meanwhile, combine 1 cup of the vinegar with the sugar and water in a large bowl and stir until the sugar is dissolved. Drain the cooked noodles, add them to the vinegar mixture, and toss to coat well. Set aside to marinate; keep warm.

HEAT THE OIL in a large skillet over high heat. Add the shrimp and cook for about 1 minute, then stir in the garlic, green onion, cilantro, and red pepper flakes. Add the wine, the remaining ¼ cup of vinegar, and the soy sauce and bring just to a boil. Add the butter pieces and stir to slowly incorporate into the sauce. Remove from the heat and taste for seasoning, adding more soy sauce or red pepper flakes to taste.

DRAIN THE WARM NOODLES, discarding the marinade, and divide them among 4 shallow bowls. Arrange the shrimp on the noodles, spoon the sauce over them, and serve immediately.

MAKES 4 SERVINGS

open ravioli of spot prawns and avocado with chilled tomato and basil consommé

WEST ◆ VANCOUVER, BRITISH COLUMBIA

Delicate homemade pasta makes this dish both impressive and delicious, but it does require a pasta machine. If you don't have access to a machine, you can try substituting store-bought lasagna noodles cut to size and quickly blanched to al dente. The elegant flavor of the broth and the sweetness of the spot prawns (which are trap-caught rather than farmed) will still delight.

Pasta Dough

1½ to 2 cups of flour, such as King Arthur Italian-style flour

Pinch salt and freshly ground black pepper

1 teaspoon extra-virgin olive oil

1 large egg

2 egg yolks

8 large fresh basil leaves, stems removed and reserved

Citrus-Marinaded Prawns

12 spot prawns

Freshly squeezed juice of 1 orange

Freshly squeezed juice of 1 lime

Zest of 1 lime

½ red chile, coarsely chopped

10 leaves cilantro, coarsely chopped

1½ tablespoons extra-virgin olive oil

Salt and freshly ground black pepper

Tomato Consommé

1 carrot, chopped

1 small onion, chopped

2 stalks celery, chopped

½ small fennel bulb, chopped

1 leek, white part only, chopped

1 clove garlic, minced

1 sprig thyme

1 bay leaf

8 ripe tomatoes, roughly chopped

1 teaspoon tomato paste

4 cups water

8 basil stems (from the leaves used in the pasta)

Clarification

1 boneless chicken breast, cut into 2-inch cubes

½ red beet, roughly chopped

½ carrot, roughly chopped

¼ medium onion, roughly chopped

1 celery stalk, roughly chopped

2 egg whites

Avacado Mixture

1 ripe avocado

Dash of Tabasco

Freshly squeezed juice of ½ lemon

Salt and freshly ground black pepper

TO MAKE THE PASTA, combine the flour, salt, and pepper in a large bowl with a fork. Make a well in the center of the flour; add the oil and eggs. Gradually pull the flour mixture into the liquid until all of the flour has been incorporated and a dough ball forms. Turn out the dough onto a lightly floured surface to knead by hand (or knead with a dough hook on an electric mixer) until the dough is smooth and elastic, adding more flour a little at a time as needed. Cover and refrigerate for at least 1 hour.

BLANCH THE BASIL LEAVES in boiling water for 5 seconds, plunge into ice water, and then dry on a paper towel.

TO MAKE THE RAVIOLI, line a tray with plastic wrap. Cut the dough into two equal parts. Leave one ball covered. Using a pasta machine set to the thickest setting, run the first ball of dough through, fold in half, and run it through again. Set the machine to the next setting and repeat with the same piece of dough. Continue to reduce the thickness of the dough sheet until it is about 2 milimeters thick. Lay the dough sheet on the work surface and cover with a towel. Repeat with the other ball of dough. Arrange the basil leaves over one of the dough sheets, then place the other half of the dough on top to sandwich the leaves. Starting from the widest setting, run the dough through the machine again, reducing the width after each pass, until the dough is ½ milimeter thick. Cut into 8 squares, 2 by 2 inches. Blanch in salted boiling water for 2 minutes, plunge into ice water, then place on the plastic-lined tray and brush gently with oil. Cover with plastic wrap and refrigerate.

TO MAKE THE CITRUS-MARINATED PRAWNS, in a large pot, blanch the prawns in salted water for 15 seconds. Peel the prawns, discarding the shells. Combine the orange juice, lime juice and zest, chile, cilantro, olive oil, salt, and pepper. Place the prawns in a shallow baking dish and pour the marinade over them. Cover and refrigerate for at least 1 hour.

TO MAKE THE TOMATO CONSOMMÉ, combine the carrot, onion, celery, fennel, leek, garlic, thyme, and bay leaf in a heavy-bottomed pan over medium heat and stir until the vegetables have softened, about 10 minutes. Add the tomatoes, cover, and cook for another 10 minutes. Stir in the tomato paste and cook for 1 minute. Add water to cover and bring to a boil. Reduce the heat to low and simmer for 45 minutes. Strain through cheesecloth and refrigerate. Discard the solids.

TO CLARIFY THE CONSOMMÉ, blend the chicken breast, beet, carrot, onion, celery, and egg whites in food processor until puréed and whisk into the chilled tomato consommé. Pour this stock into a saucepan over medium heat and stir continuously until the clarification mixture rises to the top of the stock, about 20 minutes. Break a small hole in the surface and simmer gently for another 20 minutes. Strain through cheesecloth, discarding the solids, and add the basil stems. Cover and refrigerate.

TO MAKE THE AVACADO MIXTURE, peel and pit the avocado and mash it in a bowl with a fork. Season to taste with Tabasco, lemon juice, salt, and pepper.

STRAIN THE BASIL STEMS from the tomato consommé.

TO SERVE, place 1 square of pasta in each of 4 bowls. Add a spoonful of the avocado mixture. Cut each prawn in half and place 6 pieces on top of each avocado portion. Cover with a second square of pasta. Pour the tomato consommé around each ravioli and serve.

MAKES 4 SERVINGS

sautéed razor clams with hazelnut lemon sauce

PAZZO RISTORANTE • PORTLAND, OREGON

Razor clams have a distinctive nutty sweetness that many people are passionate about. In this recipe, toasted hazelnuts accent the nutty flavor of the clams with fresh lemon and dry white wine as a contrast. This serves four as a dainty appetizer or one person as a main course.

¼ cup flour
Salt and freshly ground black pepper
4 razor clams, shucked and cleaned (about 5 ounces)
2 tablespoons olive oil
½ cup pinot gris or other dry white wine
½ teaspoon freshly squeezed lemon juice
2 tablespoons toasted, chopped hazelnuts
1 tablespoon minced shallot
¼ cup unsalted butter, cut into pieces and chilled
1 tablespoon minced flat-leaf (Italian) parsley
Flat-leaf (Italian) parsley sprigs, for garnish

MIX THE FLOUR with a pinch each of salt and pepper on a plate. Dredge the clams in the flour, patting to remove excess.

HEAT THE OIL in a medium skillet over medium-high heat. Add the clams and sauté until golden brown, about 30 seconds on each side; do not overcook. Transfer the clams to a plate and keep warm.

ADD THE WINE and lemon juice to the skillet, stirring to dissolve flavorful bits. Boil to reduce slightly, about 1 minute. Add the hazelnuts and shallot and cook for 30 seconds longer. Whisk in the cold butter until it has melted and the sauce has a rich consistency. Stir in the parsley, adding salt and pepper to taste.

ARRANGE THE CLAMS on a warm serving platter or individual plates, pour the sauce over them, and garnish with sprigs of parsley. Serve immediately.

MAKES 4 SERVINGS

steamed clams sol duc

SOL DUC HOT SPRINGS ◆ PORT ANGELES, WASHINGTON

Sol Duc Hot Springs former chef Mike Rogers won first place at the Clam Fest in Sequim, Washington, for his steamed clams. He uses Manila clams; littleneck clams are another fine choice.

3 tablespoons unsalted butter, softened
¼ cup finely chopped toasted hazelnuts
1 tablespoon hazelnut liqueur (optional)
2 tablespoons olive oil
2 tablespoons chopped sun-dried tomatoes
1 tablespoon chopped garlic
1 tablespoon chopped shallot
2 pounds Manila clams, scrubbed
¼ cup hard cider
¼ cup dry sherry
¼ cup dry white wine
Freshly squeezed juice of 1 lemon
3 tablespoons unsalted butter, cut into pieces and chilled
1 green onion, chopped
4 slices baguette, sliced diagonally and toasted

TO MAKE HAZELNUT BUTTER, combine the butter, hazelnuts, and liqueur in a small bowl. Set aside or refrigerate.

HEAT THE OIL in a large skillet over medium heat. Add the sun-dried tomatoes, garlic, and shallot and cook for 2 minutes. Add the clams, hard cider, sherry, white wine, and lemon juice. Cover and steam until the clams are open, 4 to 6 minutes. Discard any clams that do not open. Add the butter to the pan and stir gently until it has melted. Transfer the clams to individual shallow bowls, pour the sauce from the pan over them, and sprinkle each with some of the green onion. Spread the toast slices with hazelnut butter, and serve alongside the clams.

MAKES 2 TO 4 SERVINGS

northwest clams

STEAMER CLAMS

Three varieties of small, hard-shelled, sweet-tasting clams, commonly known as "steamer" or "butter" clams, are available in the Northwest. All are delicious, and they are interchangeable in recipes.

Native species include the littleneck clam (Protothaca staminea) and the Washington butter clam (Saxidomus giganteus). Littlenecks vary in color from cream to beige or gray. One variety is mottled with browns and yellows. Shells, averaging 2½ inches across, are crosshatched with growth rings crossing radiating ribs.

Washington butter clams have heavy, solid shells that are generally beige to gray in color. The shells grow from 3 to 4 inches across and are marked with concentric growth rings.

The most popular steamer clam on the market is the Manila clam (Tapes japonica), introduced to the Northwest from Asia in the 1930s. These oval-shaped clams, which range in size from 1½ to 2½ inches, have a ridged calico pattern on their shells.

Because the Manila clam cooks twice as fast as the native littleneck and butter clams (steaming time is just 3 to 4 minutes), this clam has become a favorite among Northwest chefs.

Make sure clams are alive until cooking. The shell should be shut tight or should close tightly when tapped. Stored in the refrigerator, covered with a damp cloth, live clams will keep for three to five days.

RAZOR CLAMS

Named for their oblong shell that resembles an old-fashioned straight razor, Northwest razor clams (Siliqua patula) are found along sandy ocean beaches from California to Alaska. Their sweet, succulent meat is considered a delicacy by many seafood lovers. The key to good-tasting razor clams is freshness. The flesh should smell sweet like the sea and be creamy white. There is a significant change in the odor and color of clams that have been out of the water for more than three days. If the clams smell fishy, or if the flesh has darkened, don't buy them.

flash-fried squid with herb garlic dip and horseradish gremolata

ETTA'S SEAFOOD ✻ SEATTLE, WASHINGTON

Flash-fried squid has been a favorite among Etta's Seafood customers since the day the restaurant opened. "Flash-frying," says chef Tom Douglas, "keeps squid from getting tough." To offset the intensity of the garlic dip and horseradish topping, try a distinctive Columbia pinot gris. Use any leftover herb garlic dip for a zesty sandwich spread.

Herb Garlic Dip

1 whole egg

1 egg yolk

2 tablespoons freshly squeezed lemon juice

2 tablespoons Dijon-style mustard

2 tablespoons red wine vinegar

2 cups pure olive oil (not extra-virgin)

3 tablespoons finely chopped flat-leaf (Italian) parsley

3 tablespoons finely chopped mixed herbs (such as thyme, chives, rosemary, and sage)

1½ tablespoons finely chopped garlic

Salt and freshly ground black pepper

Horseradish Gremolata

2 tablespoons chopped flat-leaf (Italian) parsley

1 tablespoon freshly grated horseradish

1½ teaspoons minced or grated lemon zest

✕

4 cups peanut oil, plus more if needed, for frying

2 to 3 cups flour

1 tablespoon paprika

1 teaspoon salt

1 teaspoon pepper

1 teaspoon dried thyme

1½ pounds cleaned squid (see page 51), tubes cut into rings

Lemon wedges, for serving

FOR THE HERB GARLIC DIP, combine the egg and egg yolk in the work bowl of a food processor. Add the lemon juice, mustard, and vinegar and process until combined. With the motor running, add the oil through the tube, drizzling it very slowly at first. Once the mixture begins to emulsify, continue adding the oil in a steady stream. Add the parsley, herbs, and garlic and pulse to combine. Season to taste with salt and pepper.

FOR THE GREMOLATA, combine the parsley, horseradish, and lemon zest in a small bowl and stir to mix. Set aside.

IN A DEEP-FRYER or large, heavy pot, heat about 3 inches of oil to 350°F. To tell when the oil is hot enough, test it by adding one coated piece of squid; it should cook golden and tender within 2 minutes.

STIR TOGETHER the flour, paprika, salt, pepper, and thyme in a shallow dish. Pat the squid dry with paper towels, add it to the seasoned flour, and toss to coat thoroughly. Remove a handful of squid and put it in a mesh sieve, tossing to remove excess flour. Use tongs to gently add the squid, piece by piece, to the hot oil and fry until golden, about 2 minutes. Scoop out the squid with a slotted spoon and let drain on paper towels. Continue with the remaining squid, shaking off excess flour and frying in batches.

ARRANGE THE SQUID on a serving platter and scatter the gremolata over it. Serve with lemon wedges for squeezing and herb garlic dip alongside for dipping.

MAKES 6 TO 8 SERVINGS

squid

There are many species of squid (also known as calamari or inkfish), but the main one sold commercially in the Northwest is Loligo opalescens, named for its opalescent flesh. The tender, cigar-shaped body of a squid is equipped with a strong beak for cutting up its feed and an internal skeleton (called a quill or pen). Ten long tentacles are attached just above its eyes. Squid also have an ink sac, from which they squirt a dark, inky (but edible) liquid to confuse and scare off predators.

Squid used in cooking are usually just 5 to 8 inches long. Once cleaned, these small squid can be sliced into rings or left whole and stuffed. Meat from larger squid is sometimes marketed as steaks; tenderize these before cooking by pounding them paper-thin with a mallet.

On the West Coast, fresh squid is available in early summer and late winter. When buying squid, look for sweet-smelling specimens with bright, shiny skin. The color should be white and purple, with no brown spots. Cleaned squid freezes well if carefully wrapped. Squid cooks quickly, becoming tough when overcooked. To prevent overcooking, test it repeatedly while cooking, carefully biting into a piece to see that it's opaque through but tender. Remove squid from the heat the instant it is done. Two pounds of whole squid will yield one and a half pounds of cleaned squid.

Cleaning squid is a very simple process but is not for the squeamish.

1. Using your fingers, peel off the mottled purple skin. Don't worry if some stubborn patches remain.

2. Pull out the head by inserting your thumb and one or two fingers into the body, below the point where the head is attached. Together with the head, pull out as many innards as possible.

3. Reach into the body and pull out the quill and any remaining innards. Use a spoon or knife to clean the body more thoroughly.

4. Rinse out the body cavity (the "tube") under cold running water. Blot dry.

5. Using a sharp knife, sever the tentacles from the head just above the beak (the hard ball located just above the squid's eyes). Reserve the edible tentacles and discard the head, beak, and innards.

6. Refrigerate cleaned squid on ice, and use within 24 hours.

northwest oysters

Few foods evoke more passion among their eaters than oysters—due no doubt in part to their reputation as the ultimate aphrodisiac. Passion aside, oysters are low in calories and high in vitamins and minerals, containing large amounts of zinc, phosphorus, iron, copper, and iodine.

Recently the Pacific Northwest surpassed the Gulf Coast region to become the top oyster-producing region in the United States. Interestingly, only one variety of oyster is indigenous to the Pacific Northwest—the tiny, coppery-flavored Olympia oyster. During the mid- to late 1800s, this oyster was in such great demand that enormous quantities from Willapa Bay and Samish Bay were shipped to restaurants in San Francisco. By the early 1900s, Olympia oysters were nearly extinct due to overharvesting and pollution. Fortunately, several Northwest companies have successfully revived the Olympia oyster industry.

Pacific oysters (native to China and Japan) are the main oyster of commerce in the Northwest today. The Kumamoto is a small variety of Pacific oyster. Local growers raise several other species of oyster, including the European flat oyster. Westcott flats, raised by Westcott Bay Sea Farms on San Juan Island, are a prime example of this species.

Oysters raised in the Northwest are often named for the area in which they are grown: Quilcene, Oysterville Specials, Hamma Hamma, Snow Creek, Skookum, Goose Point, and Fanny Bay oysters (all Pacific oysters). Like wines, oysters develop unique flavors and qualities depending on their variety and where they grow. The salinity of the water, the presence of algae or eel grass in the growing beds, and the amount of rainfall all affect an oyster's color, shape, and flavor. Different growing methods (bottom culture, raft or tray culture, and dike culture) also contribute to an oyster's flavor and texture.

During the spawning season, triggered by summer heat, oysters consume their stores of glycogen (a sweet-tasting starch), giving them energy to produce both sperm and eggs. The byproduct of this glycogen consumption is lactic acid, which gives the oysters a milky appearance and a less assertive flavor. Consequently, many people prefer to eat oysters only in cooler months, or any month with an "R," as the old adage goes.

Note: People with depressed immune systems, liver diseases, AIDS, cancer, or alcoholism should avoid eating raw oysters.

alder-grilled fanny bay oysters

SALMON HOUSE ON THE HILL ◆ WEST VANCOUVER, BRITISH COLUMBIA

In this recipe Salmon House on the Hill's former chef Dan Atkinson infuses local Fanny Bay oysters and native oyster mushrooms with the complex flavor of alder smoke. Hot from the grill, the oysters and mushrooms are drizzled with a flavorful herb vinaigrette. Note that for this recipe you will need alder chips.

3 thick slices bacon, preferably alder-smoked
¼ cup malt vinegar
2 tablespoons minced mixed herbs (such as basil, thyme, and parsley)
1 clove garlic
1 teaspoon sugar
1 teaspoon whole-grain mustard
Pinch salt
½ cup olive oil
¼ cup minced red bell pepper
¼ cup minced red onion
1 jalapeño pepper, cored, seeded, ribs removed, and very finely minced
1 teaspoon cracked black pepper
12 medium or 24 small Fanny Bay oysters in the shell
½ pound oyster mushrooms, trimmed and cleaned

PREHEAT AN OUTDOOR GRILL and soak 2 handfuls of alder chips in a bowl of water.

COOK THE BACON PIECES over the hot coals until crisp, 3 to 5 minutes. Drain well on paper towels and then cut into ¼-inch pieces and set aside. Combine the vinegar, herbs, garlic, sugar, mustard, and salt in a blender or food processor. Blend for 1 minute, then slowly add the olive oil, scraping down the sides as needed. When the oil is fully incorporated, pour the mixture into a bowl and stir in the bacon, bell pepper, onion, jalapeño, and black pepper. Set aside.

WHEN THE GRILL IS HOT, drain the wood chips well and scatter them over the coals. Set the oysters, cupped side down, on the grate, with the oyster mushrooms alongside them. Cover the grill and cook just until the oysters pop open and the mushrooms are tender, 3 to 5 minutes. Discard the top shells. Arrange the oysters and the mushrooms on individual plates. Drizzle with some of the vinaigrette, passing the rest separately. Serve immediately.

MAKES 4 SERVINGS

oyster arts

When buying oysters, look for ones with shells that are tightly closed or that close readily when tapped (that means they're alive). The meat should be tan to cream-colored, heavy and plump, with a sweet sea odor.

Store live oysters at between 34°F and 40°F. Place them flat side up in an open container and cover with a damp towel. Oysters stored this way will keep for four to seven days. Freshly shucked oyster meats should be packed in their own juices (known as the oyster's liquor), which should be clear. Stored at 34°F to 40°F, these will keep up to one week. Jarred, shucked, locally produced oysters are great for stewing, pan-frying, or baking.

To shuck oysters, the first thing you need is a good oyster knife. Many different styles are available, with short, medium, or long blades. Choose a knife that feels comfortable in your hand and that has a stainless steel blade.

1. If you will be serving the oysters raw or on the half shell, begin by preparing a plate with a bed of crushed ice to hold the opened oysters.

2. Clean the oysters thoroughly under cold running water, using a stiff brush to remove any dirt.

3. Using a folded kitchen towel to protect your hand, either cup the oyster in your hand or place it on the counter with its cupped shell down to catch the juices.

4. Using your other hand, wedge the tip of the oyster knife into the hinge of the oyster, pushing and twisting until the hinge pops.

5. Sever the adductor muscle from the top shell by sliding the oyster knife as close as possible along the inside of the upper shell.

6. Pry off the top shell.

7. Loosen the oyster from the bottom shell by running the knife under the oyster, as close as possible to the shell, and severing the bottom adductor muscle. Retain as much liquor as possible.

8. Set the shucked oysters on the crushed ice or store as described previously.

confetti garden salsa

OLYMPIC LIGHTS * FRIDAY HARBOR, WASHINGTON

At the Olympic Lights they use four different chiles in this salsa: mild, medium-hot, very hot, and super-hot. You can adjust the level of heat in this recipe by using hotter or milder chiles. The quinces they use, which come from their own trees, have a very firm, crunchy texture and lemony tart flavor. Not all quinces will be suitable for this recipe—some are too coarse and tart. Lemon juice and zest make a fine substitution.

This is a case in which chopping the vegetables by hand produces a more appealing texture than can be achieved with a food processor. Serve this salsa with chips or on grilled fish. It is best freshly made, but it will keep for up to 2 days covered in the refrigerator.

2 quinces, peeled, seeded, and minced, or the juice and grated zest of 1 lemon

2 large, ripe tomatoes, cored and minced

½ large Walla Walla Sweet onion, minced

1 yellow or red bell pepper, cored, seeded, and minced

½ pound broccoli, stems peeled if tough, minced

½ cup loosely packed flat-leaf (Italian) parsley, minced

½ cup loosely packed cilantro, minced

1 small carrot, minced

6 cloves garlic, minced

1 mild chile (such as Anaheim), cored, seeded, and minced

2 or 3 medium-hot chiles (such as jalapeño), cored, seeded, and minced

2 or 3 very hot chiles (such as serrano), cored, seeded, and minced (optional)

2 or 3 super-hot chiles (such as habanero or Thai bird), cored, seeded, and minced (optional)

Salt and freshly ground black pepper

COMBINE THE QUINCE, tomato, onion, bell pepper, broccoli, parsley, cilantro, carrot, garlic, and chiles in a large bowl. Toss to mix well, and season to taste with salt and pepper.

MAKES ABOUT 4 CUPS

APPETIZERS

stuffed walla walla sweets

GREEN GABLES INN • WALLA WALLA, WASHINGTON

Set in the heart of sweet onion country, the Green Gables Inn serves these stuffed onion appetizers bubbling over with a savory filling of sausage, bread crumbs, and cheese. The juicy sweetness of Walla Walla Sweets is enhanced by a velvety red wine brimming with dark cherry and black currant flavors, such as a Leonetti Cellar merlot.

4 medium Walla Walla Sweet onions (10 to 12 ounces each)
⅔ pound pork sausage
¾ cup bread crumbs
⅓ cup grated cheddar cheese
1 egg, lightly beaten
3 tablespoons milk
2 tablespoons chopped flat-leaf (Italian) parsley
½ teaspoon sugar
¼ teaspoon ground cinnamon
Salt and freshly ground black pepper
1 slice bacon, cut into 4 pieces (optional)

PEEL THE ONIONS and cut ½ inch off the top and bottom of each one. Bring a large pan of water to a boil, add the onions, and boil for 7 minutes. Drain the onions and let cool slightly. When cool enough to handle, remove the centers from the onions, leaving a shell of at least 3 layers. Reserve the onion centers for the stuffing. If you cannot easily push out an onion center, use a spoon to scoop out some of the flesh until the center comes free, or cut out the center with a small knife. If a shell splits, wrap a thin strip of foil around the onion to hold it together. Set the onion shells in a lightly greased baking dish.

PREHEAT THE OVEN to 350°F.

FRY THE SAUSAGE in a skillet over medium heat until no pink remains, about 10 minutes, breaking it into small pieces as it cooks. Drain well, discarding the fat.

FINELY CHOP enough of the reserved onion centers to make 2 cups. In a large bowl, combine the onion, sausage, bread crumbs, cheese, egg, milk, parsley, sugar, and cinnamon with a pinch each of salt and pepper. Mix well and stuff the mixture into the onion shells. Top each with a piece of bacon, if desired, and bake until the stuffing is very hot and the onion is tender, 30 to 40 minutes.

MAKES 4 SERVINGS

walla walla sweets

There's no doubt Northwesterners are passionate about their onions—Walla Walla Sweets, that is. From mid-June to mid-August, onion lovers flock to the small town of Walla Walla, Washington, to purchase these fragrant bulbs at roadside stands and backyard refrigerators, where you leave your money in a jar.

Celebrated all over the United States for their mild, sweet flesh, Walla Walla Sweet onions have been a favorite since the early 1900s, when they were brought to the Northwest from Italy. They are one of a handful of onion varieties that people enjoy raw, like an apple. Their flesh is sweet, crisp, and succulent without the painful sting of other onions.

Why do Walla Walla Sweets taste so sweet? It begins with the variety of seed. Soil is another important factor in determining an onion's pungency. "Our soil is a clay-mineral type that is very low in sulfur," explains Brian Magnaghi of the Walla Walla Gardeners' Association.

Sulfur-based compounds and other carbohydrates give cooking onions their powerful, tear-inducing aromas and act as natural preservatives. Walla Walla Sweets have half the sulfur content of an ordinary yellow onion.

To qualify as genuine Walla Walla Sweets, the onions must be grown within a specific geographic area, which encompasses Walla Walla County in Southwestern Washington and a small section of Umatilla County in Northeastern Oregon. Fresh Walla Walla Sweets are available only from mid-June to mid-August.

Most growers raise their own seed, which is planted during the first two weeks of September. "Onions planted in the fall develop less of the pungent sulfur compounds and are much sweeter than onions that are spring planted," explains Magnaghi. By the time the seedlings have reached the size of a small green onion, cold weather has set in, and the onions are left in the fields to winter over.

The best place to store Walla Walla Sweets is in the refrigerator. Stored in this way, they will often keep through Thanksgiving or even Christmas. For shorter-term storage, try panty hose or mesh bags, which keep air circulating around the onions. Simply put the onions, one at a time, into the legs of panty hose, tying a knot above each one. To use, snip below the lowest knot. Hung in a cool, ventilated location, Walla Walla Sweets will keep for 3 to 6 weeks.

garlic and thyme crème brûlée with chive cornmeal crackers

OCEANWOOD COUNTRY INN ⬩ MAYNE ISLAND, BRITISH COLUMBIA

Flavored with mashed, roasted garlic and fresh thyme, these pungent custards can be served alone or spread on homemade chive cornmeal crackers. The chefs at Ocean-wood Country Inn use a template to form these crackers, but you could just as easily do them freehand, spreading the batter into thin shapes.

Chive Cornmeal Crackers
⅔ cup flour
¼ cup yellow cornmeal
1 teaspoon salt
¼ teaspoon baking powder
½ cup milk, plus more if needed
2 tablespoons minced chives

✕

2 whole heads garlic
2 teaspoons olive oil
1 sprig thyme
6 egg yolks
1¼ cups whipping cream
1 tablespoon minced thyme
Salt and freshly ground black pepper

PREHEAT THE OVEN to 375°F.

CUT A RECTANGLE about 2 inches wide and 4 inches long from the middle of a sturdy piece of thin cardboard or a disposable plastic lid. The remaining border will be a template for forming the crackers.

FOR THE CRACKERS, stir together the flour, cornmeal, salt, and baking powder. Stir in the milk. The batter should be smooth and spreadable; add a little more milk if needed. Stir in the chives. Set the template on a lightly greased or parchment-lined baking sheet. With a spatula, spread the batter inside the template to form a thin rectangle, then lift off the template. Repeat with the remaining batter; you will need to

bake the crackers in batches. Bake the crackers until crisp, about 12 minutes. Carefully transfer the crackers to a wire rack to cool. Repeat with the remaining batter. Keep the oven set at 375°F.

PUT THE GARLIC HEADS on a square of foil, drizzle the olive oil over them, and set the sprig of thyme alongside the garlic. Wrap the foil snugly around the garlic and bake until soft, about 30 minutes. When cool enough to handle, peel the individual cloves of garlic and lightly mash them in a bowl. Discard the sprig of thyme. Distribute the garlic evenly among six ½-cup ramekins. Reduce the oven temperature to 300°F.

BEAT THE EGG YOLKS with the cream until well blended, then stir in the minced thyme with a pinch each of salt and pepper. Pour the mixture over the garlic in the ramekins and set them in a deep 9- by 13-inch baking pan. Add hot water to the baking pan so that it comes about halfway up the sides of the ramekins. Cover the dish with foil and bake the custards until they have just set, about 40 to 50 minutes. Remove the ramekins from the water and set aside to cool. Serve at room temperature, with the crackers on the side.

MAKES 6 SERVINGS

shiitake mushroom pâté

SYLVIA BEACH HOTEL • NEWPORT, OREGON

At the Sylvia Beach Hotel they serve this earthy pâté with Dijon mustard and home-made bread or crackers. A glass of Oregon pinot noir is a delicious accompaniment. You can substitute regular button mushrooms for half of the shiitakes.

8 ounces cream cheese, softened
½ cup sour cream
¼ cup grated Parmesan cheese
3 eggs
1 cup soft bread crumbs
2 pounds shiitake mushrooms, cleaned, trimmed, and halved
½ large onion, coarsely chopped
1 tablespoon minced garlic
2 tablespoons dried basil
1 tablespoon dried thyme
1½ teaspoons dried oregano
1½ teaspoons dried rosemary
Salt

PREHEAT THE OVEN to 350°F.

COMBINE THE CREAM CHEESE, sour cream, cheese, and eggs in a food processor and process until smooth. Put the bread crumbs in a large bowl and pour the cream cheese mixture over them. Process the mushrooms, onion, and garlic in the food processor, pulsing until they are evenly chopped; you may need to work in batches. Do not overprocess; the mushroom mixture should still be somewhat chunky. Add it to the cream cheese mixture, followed by the basil, thyme, oregano, and rosemary. Stir to mix well, adding a pinch of salt.

GENEROUSLY GREASE a 9-inch springform pan. Cut two 9-inch rounds of parchment paper and grease them. Line the bottom of the pan with one round. Spoon the mushroom mixture into the prepared pan, pressing it down evenly. Top with the remaining greased round of parchment paper, then cover the pan with foil. Bake until a knife blade inserted in the center for a few seconds comes out hot, about 1 hour. Remove the parchment paper, and serve either warm or chilled, cut into wedges.

MAKES 12 TO 16 SERVINGS

northwest wine

Each of the major wine regions in the Pacific Northwest—including wine-growing regions in Oregon, Washington, Idaho (on a small scale), and British Columbia—is renowned for producing outstanding and distinctive wines. Oregon is legendary for its elegant pinot noirs; delicate, food-friendly chardonnays; and spicy gewürztraminers and rieslings. Pinot gris, dubbed "the wine of the '90s" by some because of its mass production and popularity at the time, has continued to enjoy an increase in popularity thanks to its luscious fruit and crisp acids.

Washington State, where most grapes are grown in desert conditions east of the Cascade Mountains, has received accolades for its robust, velvety merlots and cabernet sauvignons; its luscious, rich chardonnays; and its crisp, refreshing sauvignon blancs and semillons.

To the north, British Columbia's Okanagan Valley is setting trends with distinctive varietals, including spicy, floral Ehrenfelser; fruity Maréchal Foch; and lighter reds, including Chelois and Chancellor. British Columbia also produces fine examples of pinot noir, pinot gris, riesling, and sparkling wines.

pacific northwest oyster wines

"A loaf of bread," the Walrus said,
"Is what we chiefly need:
Pepper and vinegar besides
are very good indeed—
Now, if you're ready, Oysters dear,
we can begin to feed."

"The Walrus and the Carpenter" by Lewis Carroll

The conniving, oyster-slurping Walrus in Lewis Carroll's "The Walrus and the Carpenter" certainly had his priorities straight when it came to eating oysters. Unfortunately, he and his wily colleague, the Carpenter, were negligent in assembling their picnic: they forgot the wine and, in doing so, missed one of the greatest gastronomic pleasures of all time.

Each year, Taylor Shellfish Farms sponsors the Pacific Coast Oyster Wine Competition. With the help of oyster-loving wine experts—including chefs, restaurateurs, oyster growers, and wine and food writers—the best oyster wines are selected from hundreds of submissions from wineries in British Columbia, California, Idaho, Oregon, and Washington. Each wine is tasted blind with a freshly shucked Olympia oyster on the half shell.

Overall, the judges prefer dry white wines with crisp acids that slice right through the briny, metallic flavor of the oysters. Favorite varietals include chardonnay, pinot gris, chenin blanc, sauvignon blanc, semillon, and dry riesling.

When it comes to matchmaking oysters and wine, temperature is crucial, as is freshness. Make sure both wines and oysters are ice cold. Bury oysters in ice for about an hour before shucking, and chill wines thoroughly in a refrigerator or freezer. A fresh loaf of crusty sourdough or rye bread is essential. Butter is optional. Shuck the oysters just before serving, and arrange them on a bed of crushed ice.

soups, salads & breads

creamy onion soup with bay shrimp

THE BAY HOUSE ✦ LINCOLN CITY, OREGON

Located on the banks of Siletz Bay, The Bay House has access to plenty of fresh sea-food, including the sweet, locally harvested Oregon bay shrimp in this wonderfully seasonal soup. If you can't find Walla Walla Sweets, add 1 teaspoon of sugar to the onions when caramelizing to help them accent the flavors of the sweet shrimp.

¼ cup olive oil
½ cup unsalted butter (optional, for caramelizing)
4 pounds sweet onions, preferably Walla Walla Sweets, diced
2 cups bottled clam juice
¼ cup dry white wine
¼ cup marsala
3 tablespoons uncooked basmati rice
1 teaspoon dried thyme
Salt and freshly ground black pepper
2 cups whipping cream
½ to ¾ pound cooked bay shrimp
Fresh thyme leaves, for garnish

HEAT THE OIL and butter, if using, in a large pot over medium-high heat. Add the onions and sauté until well browned and caramelized, about 30 minutes, stirring frequently. To fully caramelize the onions, which gives a distinctive flavor to this soup, you may need to cook them longer or drain off some of the liquid. Stir in the clam juice, wine, marsala, rice, and thyme with a good pinch each of salt and pepper. Bring to a boil, then reduce the heat and simmer, stirring occasionally, until the rice is very tender, about 30 minutes.

WORKING IN BATCHES, purée the soup in a food processor or blender until smooth. Return the soup to the pot and stir in the cream. Reheat the soup until very hot; taste for seasoning.

DIVIDE THE SHRIMP evenly among individual bowls. Ladle the hot soup over the shrimp and garnish each bowl with a sprinkle of thyme leaves. Serve immediately.

MAKES 4 TO 6 SERVINGS

wild mushroom and sherry bisque

STEPHANIE INN ✦ CANNON BEACH, OREGON

For a little drama, the Stephanie Inn garnishes this soup with parsley oil (made by puréeing 1 bunch of Italian parsley in a blender with ½ cup olive oil) and port syrup (made by reducing 1 bottle of port over medium heat until thickened) dispensed from squeeze bottles. You may want to simply stir in a little more sherry just before serving.

½ cup unsalted butter

½ cup flour

1½ pounds mixed wild mushrooms (such as chanterelles, boletus, oyster, and matsutake), cleaned and trimmed

3 tablespoons olive oil

1 medium onion, diced

5 cloves garlic, minced

1 teaspoon minced rosemary

1 cup dry sherry

2½ cups vegetable stock or chicken stock (see page 108)

2½ cups whipping cream

Salt and freshly ground white or black pepper

2 teaspoons minced oregano

PREPARE A ROUX by melting the butter in a small, heavy pan, stirring in the flour, and cooking over medium heat, stirring often, until the mixture forms a thick paste and has a slight toasty aroma, 4 to 5 minutes. Do not brown. Set aside to cool.

SLICE THE MUSHROOMS. Reserve about 2 cups of mixed mushrooms.

HEAT 2 TABLESPOONS of the olive oil in a large, heavy pot until very hot. Add the bulk of the mushrooms, onion, half the garlic, and the rosemary. Sauté over medium-high heat until the mushrooms are tender and the onion is lightly browned and caramelized, about 10 minutes. Add the sherry, bring to a boil, and boil to reduce the liquid by half. Add the stock and cream, return to a boil, then reduce the heat to keep the mixture at a simmer. Stir in the roux, a couple of tablespoons at a time, mixing well after each addition, until the soup is thick enough to coat the back of a spoon; you may not need all of the roux.

PASS THE SOUP through a food mill and return it to the soup pot. Alternatively, process the soup in batches in a food processor or blender; the soup should be fairly smooth but still have some texture. Season to taste with salt and pepper. Keep the soup warm over very low heat.

HEAT THE REMAINING tablespoon of oil in a medium skillet and add the reserved mushrooms with the remaining garlic and the oregano. Sauté over medium-high heat until the mushrooms are just tender and the garlic is fragrant, 3 to 4 minutes.

LADLE THE BISQUE into individual bowls and garnish each with some of the sautéed mushrooms. Serve immediately.

MAKES 6 SERVINGS

to make roux

Chef Philippe Boulot, of Portland's Heathman Hotel, offers a good lesson in roux making:

"Cook the flour and butter over low heat for approximately 6 minutes, stirring constantly and bringing the flour paste off the sides and bottom of the pan. This heated blending period is extremely important. If the temperature is too high, the flour will burn and give off a bitter flavor. If the roux is not cooked long enough, the raw taste will dominate the sauce. Finally, if there is not constant stirring, the flour will not be heated evenly and will not be able to absorb liquid well."

palouse red lentil–mint soup

CAFE LANGLEY • LANGLEY, WASHINGTON

The Palouse region of Eastern Washington, with its gently rolling hills, is renowned for red, green, and yellow lentils, which are marketed worldwide. A member of the legume family, lentils are a good source of vegetable protein. Cooked, they have a mild, nutty flavor, which is accented in this recipe by mint. Look for lentils in the bulk food section of your local supermarket; if red ones are not available, any color will work.

¼ cup unsalted butter
¾ cup chopped onion
1 tablespoon tomato paste
7 cups chicken stock (see page 108)
1 cup red lentils
2 tablespoons flour
¼ cup dried mint or ½ cup minced fresh mint
¼ teaspoon dried red pepper flakes
Salt
Croutons, for garnish (optional)

HEAT 2 TABLESPOONS of the butter in a large pot, add the onion, and sauté over medium heat until tender, 3 to 5 minutes. Stir in the tomato paste. Add the chicken stock and lentils, cover, and simmer until the lentils are tender, about 20 minutes. Remove from the heat and let cool for a few minutes. Working in batches, purée the mixture in a food processor or blender until just smooth. Set aside in a large bowl.

MELT THE REMAINING 2 tablespoons butter in the same pot over medium heat, add the flour, and whisk until the flour begins to turn golden, about 2 minutes. Gradually whisk in the lentil mixture and bring to a gentle simmer. Stir in the mint and red pepper flakes, with salt to taste, and simmer 1 to 2 minutes longer. Ladle the soup into individual bowls, garnish with croutons, if you like, and serve immediately.

MAKES 4 TO 6 SERVINGS

corn and cheese chowder

GRATEFUL BREAD BAKERY & RESTAURANT ✦ PACIFIC CITY, OREGON

Lightly spiced with cumin and spiked with sharp Tillamook cheddar cheese, this hearty soup is best when made with freshly harvested corn. Served with robust bread or muffins, it makes a satisfying lunch or light supper.

1½ pounds potatoes, peeled and cut into 1-inch dice (about 4 cups)
4 cups water
1 teaspoon cumin seed
½ cup unsalted butter
2 large onions, chopped
¼ cup flour
2½ cups half-and-half
2 cups corn kernels
Salt and freshly ground black pepper
8 to 10 ounces sharp cheddar cheese, preferably Tillamook, grated

COMBINE THE POTATOES, water, and cumin in a large pot and bring to a boil. Lower the heat and simmer until the potatoes are just tender, about 15 minutes. Do not drain the potatoes.

WHILE THE POTATOES ARE COOKING, heat the butter in a large skillet, add the onions, and cook, stirring occasionally, over medium heat until tender, about 8 to 10 minutes. Sprinkle the flour over the onions and continue cooking for a few minutes, stirring to mix well.

ADD THE ONION MIXTURE to the potatoes and their cooking water, then add the half-and-half, corn, and salt and pepper to taste. Simmer the soup until thickened, about 20 minutes, stirring occasionally.

SPRINKLE ABOUT HALF OF THE CHEESE in the bottom of individual soup bowls. Ladle the chowder over and sprinkle the remaining cheese on top. Serve immediately. Diners should stir the cheese into the soup before eating.

MAKES 6 TO 8 SERVINGS

lopez island mussel soup with saffron and cream

FRIDAY HARBOR HOUSE • SAN JUAN ISLAND, WASHINGTON

When chef Greg Atkinson was at the helm of Friday Harbor House, he planned his menu around the seasons. The hotel continues his tradition featuring local seafood when it is at its peak, like the Shoal Bay Shellfish Farm mussels from Lopez Island in this creamy soup. These mussels should only be used in the cooler months when they taste the best. During summer months look for Mediterranean mussels, which are at their prime then.

2 cups off-dry white wine, such as Lopez Island Madeleine Angevine

1 tablespoon chopped garlic

3 pounds mussels, cleaned and debearded

2 tablespoons unsalted butter

2 tablespoons flour

2 cups whipping cream

Generous pinch of saffron threads, preferably Spanish, steeped in
2 tablespoons warm water for 15 minutes

6 leaves spinach or sorrel, cut into fine ribbons, for garnish

COMBINE THE WINE and garlic in a heavy metal pot over high heat and bring to a boil. Add the mussels, cover, and steam until they begin to open, about 3 minutes. Transfer opened mussels to a bowl, using a slotted spoon. Continue steaming until all have opened, 2 to 3 minutes longer. Discard any mussels that do not open. Reserve the cooking liquid. As soon as the mussels are cool enough to handle, remove them from their shells and put them in the cooking liquid.

MELT THE BUTTER in a large saucepan. Whisk in the flour and cook, stirring, for 1 minute. Add the cream and bring to a boil, whisking constantly. Add the saffron and its steeping liquid along with the mussels and their cooking liquid. Bring the soup to a gentle boil, and serve hot, garnishing each bowl with the spinach or sorrel.

MAKES 6 SERVINGS

musselmania

Mussels have been relished in Europe for centuries. Thanks to both the emergence of a handful of quality mussel farms throughout the Northwest and the recent introduction of the winter-spawning Mediterranean mussel, they are finally catching on here.

Native to protected waters of northern Puget Sound, British Columbia, and Alaska is the **PUGET SOUND BLUE MUSSEL** (also called black or bay mussel). Similar in look and flavor to the Mediterranean mussel, but smaller, this is the mussel raised by Penn Cove Mussels of Whidbey Island, the oldest commercial mussel farm in North America.

The **WILD PACIFIC OCEAN MUSSEL** is a blue-black mussel found throughout the coastal waters of the Northwest. These mussels are hardier, with a wilder, stronger flavor.

The **MEDITERRANEAN MUSSEL** was recently discovered growing in protected bays in California and Oregon. This is the famous blue mussel of Spain, the world leader in farmed mussel production. No one is sure how these mussels found their way to the Northwest, but judging by the size of established colonies, experts speculate that they have lived here for many years, probably arriving as stowaways adhered to the bottoms of Spanish galleons. The smooth shell of these black-blue mussels has a shimmering blue interior, and the meat is sweet and succulent. Mediterranean mussels are winter spawners, meaning they are at their prime in the heat of summer.

The **EAST COAST BLUE MUSSEL**, sometimes available in Northwest markets, is currently farmed in Canada. The **GREEN-LIPPED MUSSEL** from New Zealand is also appearing in markets here.

To store mussels, place them in an open container, cover with a moist cloth, and refrigerate for up to three days. Before cooking, discard any that are not alive (the shells should be tightly closed, or should close when tapped). Also, check for "mudders" by trying to slide the two halves of the shell across each other. If they budge, the shells may be filled with mud.

Before cooking the mussels, scrub them with a stiff brush under cold water. If desired, remove the byssus, or "beard," by pulling it from the mussel with the back of a small knife or with your fingers. Pull toward the wide end of the shell. This should be done just before cooking, because mussels die once they are debearded. You can also debeard mussels after they are steamed.

mussels in corn chowder

THE INN AT LANGLEY ✦ LANGLEY, WASHINGTON

Summertime, when corn is at its peak, is the best time to make this delicious chowder, created by former innkeeper and chef Stephen Nogal for his guests at The Inn at Langley. If fresh corn is unavailable, frozen is a decent substitute. You'll want to round out the meal with lots of crusty bread, and Nogal's recommended Chinook sauvignon blanc or L'Ecole semillon makes an ideal accompaniment.

3 cups chicken stock (see page 108) or fish stock (see page 75)
1 cup dry white wine
¼ cup unsalted butter
½ cup flour
1 pound (about 4 cups) freshly cut or frozen corn kernels (thaw if frozen)
1½ cups whipping cream
Sea salt and freshly ground black pepper
2 tablespoons peanut oil
2 pounds mussels, cleaned and debearded
1 or 2 red bell peppers, cored, seeded, and diced
1 bunch flat-leaf (Italian) parsley, chopped, for garnish

BRING THE STOCK and wine to a boil in a medium saucepan, reduce the heat to low, and simmer gently. In a large, heavy pot, melt the butter over medium heat, add the flour, and whisk until the flour begins to turn golden, about 2 minutes. Whisk in about 1 cup of the hot stock and continue whisking until the mixture is very thick. Add the remaining stock, return to a boil, and simmer gently until thickened, 8 to 10 minutes. Add half of the corn and simmer 5 minutes longer. Remove from the heat.

PRESS THE MIXTURE through a food mill or sieve in batches. Do not purée in a food processor. Return the mixture to the pot, stir in the cream, and season to taste with salt and pepper. Keep hot.

HEAT THE PEANUT OIL in a wok or large skillet over medium-high heat. When the oil just begins to smoke, add the mussels and the red peppers, stirring to coat them evenly in oil. Cover the wok and cook until the first few mussels open, about

3 minutes. Pour the hot corn chowder over the mussels, stir to mix, cover, and continue cooking until all the mussels have opened, 2 to 3 minutes longer. Discard any mussels that do not open. Stir in the remaining corn and taste the soup for seasoning. Ladle the mussel chowder mixture into warmed soup bowls, sprinkle with chopped parsley, and serve.

MAKES 4 SERVINGS

basic fish stock

Fish stock takes only 20 minutes to make. White fish bones are best for making stock, halibut bones being among the best. Stock can also be made from shrimp shells peeled from raw shrimp. In many recipes, clam nectar diluted with water can be used in place of fish stock.

2 pounds fish bones, cut in pieces, and/or fish heads
1 onion, sliced
1 large carrot, sliced
2 stalks celery, sliced
Bouquet garni of 3 parsley stems, 2 thyme sprigs, and 1 bay leaf, tied
    together with string
½ teaspoon black peppercorns
6 cups water, plus more if needed

WASH THE FISH BONES and heads thoroughly in cold water; remove and discard gills if they are still present.

COMBINE THE FISH BONES, onion, carrot, celery, bouquet garni, and peppercorns in a stockpot. Add the water; it should completely cover the other ingredients. Bring slowly to a boil and simmer, uncovered, for 20 minutes. Use a large spoon to skim off scum that rises to the top.

STRAIN THE STOCK through a fine sieve or a colander lined with cheesecloth, discarding the solids. Chill and use within a few days, or freeze for up to 1 month.

Makes about 4 cups

fisherman's stew

LA SERRE RESTAURANT • YACHATS, OREGON

Featuring the catch of the day from the seaside fishing village of Yachats (pronounced "YAH-hots"), on the Oregon coast, this flavorful, tomato-based stew is brimming with Dungeness crab, freshly shucked oysters, shrimp, clams, and mussels. Serve with sourdough bread and a glass of bright, fruity pinot noir, such as Rex Hill's Kings Ridge pinot noir from Oregon.

2 to 3 tablespoons olive oil

1 onion, minced

1 stalk celery, minced

½ green bell pepper, cored, seeded, and minced

1 clove garlic, crushed

4 cups chopped ripe tomatoes (about 2 pounds) or one 28-ounce can chopped tomatoes, drained

1½ cups water

1 cup dry red wine

¼ cup tomato paste

1 bay leaf, crumbled

1 teaspoon minced oregano, or ½ teaspoon dried

1 teaspoon minced basil, or ½ teaspoon dried

1 teaspoon salt

½ teaspoon freshly ground black pepper

1½ pounds steamer clams, scrubbed

¾ pound lingcod, skin and bones removed, cut into serving pieces

1½ pounds mussels, cleaned and debearded

12 large raw shrimp, peeled and deveined

1 cooked Dungeness crab, cleaned and cracked into serving pieces

12 oysters, shucked

6 ounces cooked bay shrimp

2 tablespoons minced flat-leaf (Italian) parsley, for garnish

HEAT THE OIL in a large pot, add the onion, celery, green pepper, and garlic, and sauté over medium heat until tender and lightly browned, about 5 minutes. Add the tomatoes, water, red wine, tomato paste, bay leaf, oregano, basil, salt, and pepper. Bring just to a boil, lower the heat, cover the pot, and simmer until the sauce is thick, about 1½ hours.

ADD THE CLAMS to the pot, followed by the lingcod, mussels, and shrimp. Cover and cook over medium heat for 5 minutes. Gently stir in the crab pieces, oysters, and bay shrimp, and continue simmering until the clams and mussels have opened and the remaining seafood is cooked through, about 10 minutes longer. (If some of the seafood is cooked before the rest, remove it and set aside, covered, to keep warm.)

DIVIDE THE SEAFOOD evenly among individual bowls and pour the sauce over it. Sprinkle each serving with parsley and serve.

MAKES 6 SERVINGS

mars's oyster stew

MAPLE LEAF GRILL ✦ SEATTLE, WASHINGTON

Rich, thick, and creamy, this untraditional oyster stew from the Grill's former chef Rip Ripley is flavored with Cajun-spiced, cured tasso ham, and artichoke hearts. Ripley got the idea for this stew from his friend Margaret "Mars" Clark and named it after her. If you can't find tasso ham, substitute another ham and add a pinch of Cajun seasoning to the stew. You can shuck the oysters yourself, or use the excellent-quality oysters that are sold in jars in many areas. Look for ones labeled "extra small." When oysters aren't in season, chef Rip suggests using rock shrimp as a substitute.

2 tablespoons olive oil

1 medium onion, diced

6 ounces tasso ham, cut into julienne strips

2 teaspoons dried oregano

2 cups chicken stock (see page 108) or fish stock (see page 75)

1 cup white wine

3 cups whipping cream

2 dozen extra-small oysters, shucked

One 13-ounce can artichoke hearts, drained and quartered

1 cup spinach (about 1 ounce), cut into thin strips

3 to 4 cups steamed white rice

HEAT THE OLIVE OIL in a medium saucepan, add the onion, and sauté over medium-high heat until softened but not browned, 3 to 5 minutes. Add the ham and oregano and sauté for 1 minute longer. Add the stock and wine, bring to a boil, and boil until reduced by about two-thirds (down to about 1 cup), 10 to 12 minutes. Add the cream and return to a boil. Add the oysters and artichoke hearts, reduce the heat, and simmer until the oysters plump and the edges begin to curl, about 3 minutes.

DIVIDE THE SPINACH among 4 individual bowls, and ladle the oyster stew over it. Serve the steamed rice on the side.

MAKES 4 SERVINGS

northwest caesar salad

COLOPHON CAFE ❀ BELLINGHAM, WASHINGTON

Lighter and easier to prepare than the classic Caesar salad, this variation is made without the raw egg used in most Caesar dressings. You could substitute sautéed squid or scallops for the shrimp or smoked salmon.

4 cups cubed day-old bread

½ cup unsalted butter, melted

4 or 5 cloves garlic, minced

1 teaspoon thyme leaves

1 teaspoon minced flat-leaf (Italian) parsley

1 teaspoon minced tarragon

½ cup olive oil

1 tablespoon freshly squeezed lemon juice, plus more to taste

2 teaspoons Worcestershire sauce

1 teaspoon Dijon-style mustard

Salt and freshly ground black pepper

1 small head romaine lettuce, rinsed and dried

1 small head green-leaf lettuce, rinsed and dried

¼ cup grated Parmesan cheese

1 cup cooked shrimp or flaked smoked salmon (about 6 ounces)

TO MAKE CROUTONS, preheat the oven to 325°F. Scatter the bread cubes in an even layer on a baking sheet. In a small bowl, combine the butter, 1 teaspoon of the minced garlic, thyme, parsley, and tarragon. Drizzle the butter mixture over the bread cubes and stir to evenly coat the bread. Bake for about 18 minutes, stirring once after 8 minutes, until nicely browned and crunchy. Set aside to cool.

MEANWHILE, combine the olive oil, remaining garlic, lemon juice, Worcestershire sauce, mustard, and salt and pepper to taste in a jar with a tight-fitting lid and shake well to mix.

TEAR THE ROMAINE and green-leaf lettuce into large pieces and put them in a large bowl. Add the Parmesan cheese, shrimp, and cooled croutons and toss. Shake the dressing to mix, drizzle it over the salad, and toss to coat well. Serve immediately.

MAKES 2 TO 4 SERVINGS

spinach salad

DELILAH'S • VANCOUVER, BRITISH COLUMBIA

At Delilah's they top this piquant salad with grilled peppers just before serving. You can also use roasted bell peppers from a jar, or fresh bell peppers, as we do here. Filled with beans, feta cheese, and fried pancetta, the salad is hearty enough to be served as a main dish.

⅓ cup olive oil

2 tablespoons balsamic vinegar

1½ teaspoons minced basil

½ teaspoon Dijon-style mustard

Salt and freshly ground black pepper

2 tablespoons diced pancetta or bacon

1 bunch spinach, tough stems removed

½ cup cooked white beans (canned or freshly cooked)

2 tablespoons crumbled feta cheese

2 tablespoons pine nuts, toasted

¼ red bell pepper, cored, seeded, and diced

¼ yellow bell pepper, cored, seeded, and diced

FOR THE DRESSING, combine the oil, vinegar, basil, and mustard in a small bowl and whisk to mix. Add salt and pepper to taste and set aside.

FRY THE PANCETTA in a small skillet until crisp. In a large bowl, combine the spinach, beans, feta, pine nuts, pancetta, and bell peppers. Drizzle the vinaigrette over the salad and toss to mix well. Arrange the salad on individual plates, distributing the ingredients as evenly as possible. Serve immediately.

MAKES 4 SERVINGS

frisée with red beets and blue cheese

MARCO'S SUPPERCLUB ❖ SEATTLE, WASHINGTON

No food smacks of the sweet earth more than tender cooked beets. Here they're combined with slightly bitter frisée greens and tangy blue cheese. For best results, wrap the beet in foil and roast in a 400°F oven for about 1 hour, or until tender. You can also boil the beet for about 30 minutes. When frisée isn't available, this salad is also delicious made with escarole or romaine lettuce.

1 cooked medium red beet (about 10 ounces), peeled, trimmed, and
  cut into julienne strips
1 tablespoon cider vinegar
1 tablespoon minced mint
2 teaspoons minced shallots
2 teaspoons sugar
Salt and freshly ground black pepper

Sherry Vinaigrette
2 tablespoons pure olive oil
1 tablespoon extra-virgin olive oil
1 tablespoon sherry vinegar
1 teaspoon minced shallot
1 teaspoon Dijon-style mustard
1 teaspoon minced thyme

✕

1 or 2 heads baby frisée greens, rinsed and torn into large pieces
¼ cup crumbled blue cheese, plus more to taste

COMBINE THE BEETS, vinegar, mint, shallots, and sugar with a pinch each of salt and pepper in a bowl and toss to mix well. Set aside for 1 hour, or cover and refrigerate for up to 1 day.

FOR THE VINAIGRETTE, combine the oils, vinegar, shallot, mustard, and thyme in a small bowl and whisk to mix. Season to taste with salt and pepper.

COMBINE THE FRISÉE and beets in a large bowl. Pour the vinaigrette over the salad and toss to mix well. Arrange on individual plates, sprinkle the blue cheese over the salad, and serve.

MAKES 4 SERVINGS

endive and hood river apples with spiced pecans, goat cheese, and sherry vinaigrette

RIVERPLACE HOTEL • PORTLAND, OREGON

Noted for its slightly bitter, nutty flavor, Belgian endive (or witloof chicory) is a small, cone-shaped salad green with slender 5- to 6-inch leaves that are tightly packed. Look for creamy white leaves with pale yellow tips and no blemishes. The chef at RiverPlace suggests experimenting with different goat cheeses, as they all have different characters. Also, he recommends seeking out the oldest sherry vinegar you can find, as these vinegars mellow with age.

Spiced Pecans

1 tablespoon unsalted butter
1 tablespoon honey
½ teaspoon ground coriander
½ teaspoon ground fennel seed
½ teaspoon ground cardamom
¼ teaspoon ground cinnamon
¼ teaspoon ground mace
¼ teaspoon salt
⅛ teaspoon ground cayenne
⅛ teaspoon ground cloves
4 ounces pecan pieces

Sherry Vinaigrette

¼ cup walnut oil
¼ cup vegetable oil
2 tablespoons aged sherry vinegar
2 tablespoons freshly squeezed orange juice
Salt and freshly ground white or black pepper

✂

6 heads Belgian endive (about 1½ pounds)
2 red apples, preferably Gala or Fuji, cored and cut into thin strips
6 ounces goat cheese, crumbled
Crushed pink peppercorns, for garnish
Minced chives, for garnish

FOR THE PECANS, preheat the oven to 350°F. Melt the butter with the honey in a small saucepan and stir in the coriander, fennel seed, cardamom, cinnamon, mace, salt, cayenne, and cloves. Add the pecan pieces and stir until thoroughly coated in the spice mixture. Spread the pecans evenly on a nonstick or lightly greased baking sheet. Bake until the nuts are crisp, 12 to 15 minutes. Set aside to cool.

FOR THE VINAIGRETTE, combine the walnut oil, vegetable oil, vinegar, and orange juice in a small bowl. Whisk to mix well, then add salt and pepper to taste. Set aside.

TRIM THE CORES from the endive and remove three large outer leaves from each head. Arrange three of the leaves, like the spokes of a wheel, on each of 6 plates. Cut the remaining endive into julienne strips and put it in a large bowl with the apples, goat cheese, and spiced pecans.

WHISK THE VINAIGRETTE to mix, then pour about ⅓ cup of it over the endive mixture. Toss to mix well so that some of the goat cheese blends with the vinaigrette to thicken it slightly (the chef suggests using your hands to toss the salad). Taste the salad for seasoning, adding more dressing to taste. Pile some of the salad in the center of each plate. Sprinkle the crushed peppercorns and chives over the salad and serve.

MAKES 6 SERVINGS

an apple a day

If you followed the age-old advice and ate an apple a day, sampling a new variety each day, it would take at least twenty-seven years to taste the ten thousand or more varieties of apples that exist. Chances are you would never run out of apples.

"Apples are like roses," says apple grower Alan Foster of Newberg, Oregon. "There is unlimited potential for breeding apples, so we'll never run out of new varieties."

Washington State leads the country in apple production, bringing in between 80 and 103 million boxes of the fruit each year. Stacked one on one, they would circle the earth twelve times.

Although more than twenty apple varieties are grown commercially in Washington, two of every three apples grown in the state are Red Delicious. To please consumers, growers continued breeding redder and redder Red Delicious apples. "Unfortunately, in our zeal for producing the most beautiful apple, we forgot about the most important part—taste!" says apple grower Dick Olsen, who, with his brother Larry, owns 18,000 acres of farmland in Prosser, Washington.

Although Olsen believes that Red Delicious will remain king of the apples for the next ten or more years, he and his brother are also looking toward the future by growing and marketing different varieties. They have planted half of their orchards in so-called new or exotic apples— Fuji, Gala, Elstar, Braeburn, and Criterion. "Fujis are so spectacular, they are bound to replace some older varieties," says Larry Olsen. "They are great for eating or cooking, store extremely well, and will win converts easily on their quality alone."

The Olsens recommend storing apples in the refrigerator. Other growers suggest wrapping apples individually in newspaper and storing them in a cool place at uniform temperature, either in the refrigerator or in an unheated basement.

green papaya salad

WILD GINGER ✦ SEATTLE, WASHINGTON

This traditional salad gets its fresh and spicy flavor from several herbs that you can find in Asian supermarkets. The herbs go by many names, so finding them may be a treasure hunt. Perilla (Perilla frutescens), *a minty Japanese leaf, may also be known by the Japanese name* shiso. *The long, grasslike laksa leaves* (Persicaria odorata) *may also be known by the Vietnamese name,* rau ram, *or as Vietnamese or Cambodian mint. Saw tooth leaf* (Eryngium foetidum) *is also known as Mexican coriander, and although different from the leafy cilantro readily available in most markets, the latter has a similar enough flavor that you can use it as a substitute.*

1 tablespoon palm sugar

2 tablespoons water

1 clove garlic, minced

3 fresh bird chiles, seeds removed

Freshly squeezed juice of 2 medium limes

4 tablespoons fish sauce

1 tablespoon vegetable oil

1 shallot, sliced

1 large green papaya

1 carrot, peeled and shredded

1 tablespoon Thai basil, coarsely chopped

1 tablespoon *shiso* leaves, coarsely chopped

2 tablespoons *rau ram* or laksa leaves, coarsely chopped

1 tablespoon saw tooth leaves, coarsely chopped

FOR THE DRESSING, dissolve the palm sugar in the water in a small bowl. Pound the garlic and chiles with a mortar and pestle to make a coarse paste. Add the garlic-chile mixture to the sugar water, then whisk in the lime juice and fish sauce. Cover and set aside.

COVER A PLATE with a paper towel. In a small skillet, heat the oil over medium-high heat until just before it starts to smoke. Add the shallot and fry until golden, 2 to 3 minutes. Remove with a slotted spoon and drain on the paper towel.

PEEL AND SHRED the green papaya with a box grater or mandolin. Wrap the grated papaya in cheesecloth and squeeze out any water, then place the papaya in a large bowl. Add the carrot, basil, *shiso*, *rau ram*, and saw tooth and toss until well combined.

TO SERVE, add dressing to taste and top with the fried shallots.

MAKES 4 TO 6 SERVINGS

warm bean salad with lamb

CHRISTINA'S ◆ ORCAS ISLAND, WASHINGTON

Tossed with winter greens, this nourishing salad makes a delicious lunch or dinner, especially served with a glass of velvety-rich Hogue Cellars merlot. This is a great use of leftover lamb—or substitute chicken, duck, or roast beef.

1¼ cups dry beans, preferably appaloosa, chestnut, cannellini, or other heritage beans

Vinaigrette
⅓ cup sherry vinegar
1 clove garlic, minced
1 teaspoon thyme leaves
1 teaspoon chopped chives
1 teaspoon minced sage
1 cup pure olive oil (not extra-virgin)
Salt and freshly ground black pepper

✕

1 red bell pepper
1 small red onion, halved and thinly sliced
1 fennel bulb, trimmed, cored, and thinly sliced
¾ pound cooked lamb, shredded
4 to 6 cups mixed winter greens (such as arugula, frisée, and escarole), torn into large pieces
Radicchio and sage leaves, for garnish

PUT THE BEANS in a large bowl and pour boiling water over to cover by 1 inch. Let sit for 1 hour, then drain the beans and put them in a saucepan with fresh, cold water to cover by 2 inches. Bring to a boil, reduce the heat, and simmer until the beans are tender, about 30 minutes, adding more boiling water if necessary to keep the beans completely covered. Drain the beans and set aside.

FOR THE VINAIGRETTE, whisk together the vinegar, garlic, thyme, chives, and sage. Whisk in the olive oil and season to taste with salt and pepper. Set aside.

ROAST THE RED PEPPER over a gas flame or under the broiler, turning often, until evenly charred. Put the pepper in a paper or plastic bag, close the bag, and let sit until cool enough to handle. Remove the skin, then halve the pepper, discarding the core and seeds. Cut the pepper into thin strips and set aside.

PREHEAT THE OVEN to 400°F.

COMBINE THE BEANS, roasted bell pepper, onion, fennel, and lamb in a large stainless steel bowl. Whisk the vinaigrette to remix and pour about ½ cup of it over the bean mixture. Toss to mix, then put the bowl in the oven for 8 to 12 minutes.

REMOVE THE BOWL from the oven, add the greens, and toss until they are mixed into the salad and have wilted. Taste the salad for seasoning, adding more dressing, salt, or pepper to taste. Immediately arrange the salad on individual plates, with the greens toward the bottom and other ingredients on top. Garnish the plates with radicchio and sage leaves and serve immediately.

MAKES 4 TO 6 SERVINGS

dungeness crab with ocean salad

This crab salad from chef Thierry Rautureau resounds with the flavors of the briny sea. It is made with ocean salad (a toss of fresh edible seaweeds marinated in sesame oil, chiles, mirin, and soy sauce), which is available, premixed, at some grocery stores and seafood markets. Or try fresh steamed asparagus tossed with vinaigrette as a side.

Horseradish Aioli

2 egg yolks

2 cloves garlic, minced

1½ teaspoons Dijon-style mustard

1½ teaspoons prepared horseradish

½ cup extra-virgin olive oil

1 tablespoon minced chives

1 tablespoon vinegar

Salt and freshly ground black pepper

2 cups (about ¾ pound) Dungeness crabmeat

7 ounces ocean salad

½ red bell pepper, cored, seeded, and finely diced

½ yellow bell pepper, cored, seeded, and finely diced

¼ pound snow peas, blanched, drained, and thinly sliced

1 tablespoon minced shallot

FOR THE AIOLI, combine the egg yolks, garlic, mustard, and horseradish in a food processor. With the machine running, add the oil, drizzling it very slowly at first. Once the mixture begins to emulsify, continue adding the oil in a steady stream. Add the chives, vinegar, and salt and pepper to taste. Set aside.

REMOVE ANY BITS OF SHELL or cartilage from the crabmeat. Coarsely chop enough of the ocean salad to make 3 tablespoons; set the rest aside.

COMBINE THE CRABMEAT, chopped ocean salad, bell peppers, snow peas, and shallot in a large bowl. Toss to mix well, and season to taste with salt and pepper.

ARRANGE THE CRAB SALAD in mounds on individual plates, placing the remaining ocean salad alongside it. Drizzle with the horseradish aioli and serve.

MAKES 6 TO 8 SERVINGS

dungeness crab

Many seafood lovers consider sweet, buttery-rich Dungeness crab to be the best eating crab in the world. "Dungeness crab," said James Beard, "is sheer unadulterated crab heaven."

The range of this succulent crustacean extends from Monterey Bay in California north to Alaska. Dungeness crab is available most of the year. The largest Dungeness crabs are taken from Alaskan waters, where the minimum catch standard is 6¼ inches across the shell. Only male crabs may be harvested.

Dungeness crabs are sold live, cooked, or cooked and frozen. Whenever possible, buy live rather than precooked crab; your chances of getting a better-quality product are much greater, because commercial crab cookers cook all crabs for the same amount of time, regardless of their weight, overcooking all but the largest crabs.

Live crabs should be purchased within one week of harvest and cooked the same day you buy them. Chill them thoroughly before cooking by packing them in ice and covering them with a damp towel. (If crabs are warm when you drop them into boiling water, they are more likely to drop a leg or two.) Chilled crabs become sluggish, but they should still move their legs and mouths when provoked.

BUYING DUNGENESS CRAB

When buying Dungeness crab, be selective. Use your senses to find the freshest ones available.

LOOK: The legs and shell should all be intact. The crab's shell should be clean, brightly colored, and free from cracks or punctures. Live crabs should be violet and beige. Cooked crabs should be bright red.

TOUCH: The crab should feel heavy for its size (this means that the meat fills the shell). The shell should feel hard (soft shells mean that the crab has not finished molting). Feel the back of cooked crabs to make sure they are very cold; otherwise unwanted bacteria may have started to grow.

LISTEN: Tap the shell; the crab should sound firm and solid, not hollow.

SMELL: *Fresh or cooked crabs should smell sweet and clean, like the ocean. Older crabs will smell like sweaty tennis shoes or, worse, ammonia.*

TASTE: *If the crab is precooked, ask to sample a leg. The meat should taste sweet and clean and should not be too salty.*

COOKING DUNGENESS CRAB

Cook crabs in boiling sea water or salt water (½ pound of kosher salt per gallon of water gives the same salinity as sea water) for 8 to 10 minutes per pound. Once the crabs are cooked, transfer them immediately to a sink or bowl filled with ice water, and chill thoroughly before serving. Eat fresh crab within three days of cooking.

To clean the cooked crab, first pry off the top shell. Then remove the V-shaped abdominal shield or "apron" from the underside of the crab. Holding the crab under cold running water, use your thumbs to scrape away the gills and liver from the sides of the crab cavity.

Anyone who's been frustrated trying to crack crab using a nutcracker will be happy to learn there's a much more efficient way—with a mallet. Using your hands, break the crab body into two halves. Remove the legs and claws from the body. Crack the body sections by placing them on a firm surface and crushing them under the palm of your hand. Using a wooden or metal mallet, crack each claw section by placing the claw, edge side up, over the center of a double sink or on a board and striking firmly with the mallet to split the shell (do not strike so hard that you crush the meat). Crack each leg gently, holding them on edge.

When serving Dungeness crab, allow ½ to 1 whole crab per person. Clean and precrack crabs and serve with melted butter or with your favorite sauce.

Cover the table with butcher paper or layers of newspaper and have plenty of napkins on hand. Finger bowls filled with hot tea and lemon slices will clean sticky fingers admirably (the tannin from the tea and acid from the lemon cut right through the fat in the crab). And have hot towels available for wiping hands. Once the table is set, tie on a bib, roll up your sleeves, and dive in.

kale, apple, and fresh scallop salad

SOOKE HARBOUR HOUSE ♦ SOOKE, BRITISH COLUMBIA

The Sooke Harbour House has made a name for itself designing dishes from seasonal ingredients found mere steps away from their front door. This hearty salad breathes new life into the winter dinner table when you might otherwise think that there is no fresh produce to be found. If you can, use sweet, tender jumbo scallops like the Weathervane or the purple-hinged rock varieties that are plentiful in the Pacific Northwest.

3 tablespoons blueberry or raspberry vinegar

5 tablespoons olive oil

1 teaspoon Dijon or Meaux mustard

1 tablespoon heavy cream

4 cups curly or flat-leaf kale, rinsed and torn into bite-size pieces (tough stems discarded)

2 tablespoons unsalted butter

2 Granny Smith apples, cored and cut into 8 slices each

½ pound fresh jumbo scallops, sliced into ½ inch rounds

FOR THE VINAIGRETTE, whisk together the vinegar and oil in a small bowl. Add the mustard, and whisk until the ingredients emulsify and thicken. Add the cream, mix well, and set aside.

BLANCH THE KALE LEAVES in boiling water for 15 seconds. Drain and immediately plunge into ice water. Gently pat the leaves dry and set aside.

MELT 1 TABLESPOON of the butter in a small frying pan over medium-high heat. Add the apples and sauté until they are slightly softened and golden, 5 to 10 minutes. Remove from the pan and keep warm.

MELT THE REMAINING BUTTER in the same pan over medium-high heat, add the scallops, and sauté until they lose their translucence, about 3 minutes. Remove from heat.

ARRANGE THE KALE on 4 salad plates. Evenly divide the apple slices among the plates, top with the scallops, and pour the vinaigrette over all.

MAKES 4 SERVINGS

beyond the big three

Red Delicious, Golden Delicious, and Granny Smith are the big sellers in the Northwest, but our markets offer many less-familiar varieties. Here are just a few you might like to try.

FUJI: Developed in Japan in the 1930s, Fuji is a cross between Red Delicious and Ralls Janet. It is red with a green to yellow background. The flesh is firm, crisp, and juicy, with sweet apple and pear notes. Fuji retains its shape well during cooking and is also good eaten fresh or in salads.

GALA: Developed in New Zealand in 1939 from parent varieties Kidd's Orange and Golden Delicious, this apple is pale to golden yellow with red stripes or blush. Its flavor is sweet and aromatic, and it has a firm, crisp texture. Galas are recommended for fresh eating and for applesauce and desserts.

BRAEBURN: Discovered as a chance seedling in New Zealand in 1952, Braeburn is believed to be a cross between Granny Smith and Lady Hamilton. The color ranges from red blush on a green background to all red. The flavor is mildly sweet/tart, with intense flavor and good aromatics. Firm, crisp, and juicy, Braeburn is recommended for eating fresh as well as for cooking.

JONAGOLD: This cross between Golden Delicious and Jonathan was developed in New York in the 1960s. The round to conical fruit is bright red over gold, has a moderately sweet/tart flavor, and is firm and crisp. Jonagold is wonderful in salads and for cooking and baking.

Other varieties sometimes found in Northwest markets include Gravenstein (a crisp, acidic early-ripening older variety) and Spartan (a cross between McIntosh and Yellow Newtown Pippin).

tomato cheddar dill bread

ABIGAIL'S HOTEL ❖ VICTORIA, BRITISH COLUMBIA

Abigail's serves this beautiful, tangy bread for breakfast. You'll get the accolades if you offer it at your next brunch.

2 cups flour
1 cup grated cheddar cheese
1½ teaspoons baking powder
1 teaspoon salt
½ teaspoon baking soda
1 cup puréed tomato (fresh or canned)
¾ cup minced onion
¼ cup minced fresh dill, or 1 tablespoon dried
¼ cup vegetable oil
2 eggs

PREHEAT THE OVEN to 375°F. Lightly grease a 5- by 9-inch loaf pan.

STIR TOGETHER the flour, cheese, baking powder, salt, and baking soda in a large bowl. In another bowl, combine the puréed tomato, onion, dill, oil, and eggs. Add this mixture to the dry ingredients and stir just until thoroughly blended. Pour the batter into the loaf pan and bake until the bread is nicely browned and a toothpick inserted in the center comes out clean, 50 to 55 minutes. Turn the bread onto a wire rack to cool before cutting.

MAKES 1 LOAF

hazelnut and onion bread

COLUMBIA GORGE HOTEL ✦ HOOD RIVER, OREGON

Flavored with onions and hazelnuts, this savory loaf is delicious spread with butter, or served with local cheeses and a glass of Oregon pinot noir.

3 cups bread flour
½ cup chopped toasted hazelnuts
3 tablespoons canola oil
¼ cup finely chopped onion
2 teaspoons onion powder
1½ teaspoons salt
¾ teaspoon sugar
1½ tablespoons (1½ packages) active dry yeast
1 cup warm water

COMBINE THE FLOUR, hazelnuts, oil, onion, onion powder, salt, and sugar in the large bowl of an electric mixer and stir. Sprinkle the yeast over the warm water in a small bowl and let sit until the yeast dissolves and the mixture begins to bubble, 2 to 3 minutes. Pour the water and yeast mixture into the flour mixture and mix with a dough hook or a wooden spoon until thoroughly combined, about 6 minutes. Continue kneading the dough until smooth and supple, a few minutes longer. Place the dough in a lightly oiled bowl, cover with a warm, damp cloth, and let rise in a warm place until doubled in bulk, about 1 hour.

PUT THE DOUGH on a lightly floured work surface. Flatten the dough into a rectangle, removing all air bubbles. Roll the dough tightly into a cylinder. Use your hands to gently taper and round the ends; the loaf should have an elongated, oval shape. Place the loaf on a baking sheet, seam side down, and let rise until doubled, about 1 hour longer.

PREHEAT THE OVEN to 350°F.

JUST BEFORE BAKING, make a shallow lengthwise slit in the top of the loaf with a sharp knife. Brush the loaf with water and bake until the bread is nicely browned, about 40 minutes.

MAKES 1 LOAF

you say hazelnut . . . and i say filbert

In Europe the hazelnut is also called the filbert or the cobnut. The former name honors St. Philibert, a seventh-century abbot whose feast day, August 22, falls when the nuts are ripening. In the United States, some people call them hazelnuts and others call them filberts. Whatever name you choose for them, they are a delicacy.

Ninety-eight percent of the hazelnuts raised in the United States are grown in Oregon's Willamette Valley; the other 2 percent come from southwestern Washington. Oregon hazelnuts, which make up 3 percent of the world's production, are renowned for their extremely large size and exceptional flavor. An English sailor planted the first cultivated hazelnut tree in 1858 in Oregon's Umpqua Valley. The tree still stands today.

Hazelnuts are harvested in the fall, when the air is brisk and the leaves dazzle the eye. These bushy shrubs and trees are native to the temperate regions of the Northern Hemisphere, including Europe and the Pacific Northwest. Because the nuts of the wild hazels indigenous to the Pacific Northwest are quite small, the hazelnuts favored for cultivation are European species. The three hazelnut varieties raised commercially in Oregon are Barcelona (the most common variety), Ennis, and Daviana.

Like all nuts, hazelnuts are a good source of B vitamins, protein, fat, and fiber; they are especially rich in vitamin E, copper, and magnesium. Roasted hazelnuts have an alluring, sweet, toasty aroma; a buttery, rich flavor; and an addictive crunch.

TOASTING HAZELNUTS AND OTHER NUTS

Preheat the oven to 350°F. Distribute shelled nuts evenly over a baking pan in a single layer. Roast in the oven, stirring occasionally, until the nuts are golden brown and fragrant. The time needed will depend on the size and variety of the nut. Most nuts will toast in about 10 minutes. Smaller nuts or small pieces will toast more quickly. Overtoasting will give nuts an unpleasant bitter flavor.

To remove the papery skins from roasted hazelnuts, gather the nuts in a dish towel and rub briskly between layers of the towel.

fairburn peasant bread

FAIRBURN FARM COUNTRY MANOR ✴ DUNCAN, BRITISH COLUMBIA

The Fairburn Farm Country Manor is an organic farm operating since 1955, with a history of growing and grinding their own wheat. Brimming with the nutty sweetness of fresh whole wheat flour and rolled oats, this hearty bread is great with soup or cheese.

¾ teaspoon sugar

2⅔ cups lukewarm water

1½ tablespoons (1½ packages) active dry yeast

⅓ cup unsalted butter, melted, or vegetable oil

⅓ cup packed brown sugar or honey

2 teaspoons molasses

2 teaspoons salt

1⅓ cups rolled oats, plus more for pans

6 to 7 cups whole wheat flour, or half whole wheat flour and half
  unbleached all-purpose flour

DISSOLVE THE SUGAR in 1 cup of the lukewarm water in a large bowl and sprinkle the yeast over it. Let sit until bubbly, 5 to 10 minutes, then stir to mix well. Add the remaining 1⅔ cups water with the butter, brown sugar, molasses, and salt; stir to mix. Stir in the oats, followed by the flour, 1 cup at a time. When the dough is firm, turn it onto a lightly floured work surface and knead until it is smooth and supple, about 10 minutes. Put the dough in a lightly oiled bowl, turning to evenly coat it in oil. Cover with a cloth and let rise in a warm place until doubled in bulk, about 1½ hours.

TURN THE DOUGH OUT onto a lightly oiled surface and punch it down. Grease two 5- by 9-inch loaf pans and sprinkle the insides sparingly with some oats. Divide the dough in half and shape each into a cylinder that fits snugly in the pan. Put the loaves in the pans, cover with a cloth, and let rise in a warm place until doubled and the loaf tops are rounded and smooth, about 1 hour.

PREHEAT THE OVEN to 400°F. Bake the loaves for 20 minutes, reduce the heat to 350°F, and continue baking until the loaves are browned, 15 to 20 minutes longer. To check for doneness, tip one loaf carefully from the pan and tap the bottom of the loaf with your fingers; it should sound hollow. Turn the loaves out onto a wire rack to cool, with a cloth over them to help keep the crust soft.

MAKES 2 LOAVES

lemon thyme zucchini bread

FAIRMONT CHATEAU WHISTLER ◆ WHISTLER, BRITISH COLUMBIA

Here's a zucchini loaf delicately perfumed with fresh lemon thyme. It's ideal with an afternoon cup of tea or coffee. Lemon thyme, a tiny perennial herbaceous shrub of the mint family, grows extremely well in the Pacific Northwest. With its colorful variegated foliage, it makes a lovely addition to a window box or garden.

3 cups flour
¾ cup raisins
1 tablespoon ground cinnamon
1 teaspoon ground nutmeg
1 teaspoon baking soda
1 teaspoon baking powder
½ teaspoon salt
2 whole eggs, or 4 egg whites
1 cup packed brown sugar
¾ cup plain low-fat yogurt
⅓ cup vegetable oil
¼ cup milk
2 teaspoons vanilla extract
2 cups finely grated unpeeled zucchini (about 1 medium zucchini)
Leaves from 2 bunches lemon thyme (about ½ cup)

PREHEAT THE OVEN to 350°F. Lightly grease a 5- by 9-inch loaf pan.

STIR TOGETHER the flour, raisins, cinnamon, nutmeg, baking soda, baking powder, and salt. In a large bowl, whip the eggs or egg whites until frothy, then stir in the brown sugar, yogurt, oil, milk, and vanilla. Stir in the zucchini and lemon thyme.

ADD THE DRY INGREDIENTS to the zucchini mixture and stir gently just until thoroughly combined. Pour the batter into the prepared loaf pan and bake until a toothpick inserted in the center comes out clean, 55 to 65 minutes. Turn the bread onto a wire rack and let cool before slicing.

MAKES 1 LOAF

main dishes

poulet aux crevettes
(chicken with shrimp)

CHARLES AT SMUGGLERS COVE ✦ MUKILTEO, WASHINGTON

Exciting tales of bootlegging and smuggling surround this restaurant, which was built in 1929 and was formerly a speakeasy and distillery. Today, the excitement here lies in Northwest ingredients cooked in traditional French ways. This innovative take on a classic chicken dish is made with a sauce composed of shrimp, cream, tomatoes, and white wine. Serve with steamed rice.

4 boneless, skinless chicken breasts (about 6 ounces each)
Salt and freshly ground black pepper
¼ cup flour
2 tablespoons unsalted butter
4 ounces medium shrimp, peeled and deveined
½ cup diced tomato
½ cup dry white wine
½ cup whipping cream
2 shallots, minced
2 cloves garlic, minced
2 tablespoons minced flat-leaf (Italian) parsley

PREHEAT THE OVEN to 375°F.

LIGHTLY SEASON the chicken breasts with salt and pepper. Coat each in flour, patting to remove excess. Heat the butter in a sauté pan or ovenproof skillet, add the chicken breasts, and cook over medium-high heat until well browned, 2 to 3 minutes on each side. Spoon off and discard excess butter from the pan; add the shrimp, tomato, wine, cream, shallots, and garlic. Put the pan in the oven and bake until the chicken is just cooked through, about 15 minutes. Transfer the chicken to individual warmed plates and season the sauce to taste with salt and pepper. Spoon the shrimp and sauce over the chicken, sprinkle each plate with parsley, and serve immediately.

MAKES 4 SERVINGS

hazelnut chicken breasts with berry sauce

GIRAFFE RESTAURANT • WHITE ROCK, BRITISH COLUMBIA

Former chef-owner Corinne Poole dreamed up this Northwest dish while sitting on a beach in Hawaii, feeling homesick for British Columbia. At the restaurant, she served it with grilled asparagus drizzled with a balsamic vinaigrette.

4 boneless, skinless chicken breasts (about 6 ounces each)
1 tablespoon Dijon-style mustard
2 teaspoons minced fresh herbs (such as marjoram, oregano, thyme, and parsley)
Salt and freshly ground black pepper
1 cup flour
1 egg
2 tablespoons milk
1 cup coarsely ground hazelnuts

Berry Sauce
1 cup blackberries (fresh or unsweetened frozen)
1 cup raspberries (fresh or unsweetened frozen)
½ cup water
2 shallots, minced
3 tablespoons raspberry vinegar or red wine vinegar
3 tablespoons crème de cassis (black currant liqueur) (optional)
1 tablespoon sugar

LAY THE CHICKEN BREASTS in a dish and spread them evenly with mustard. Sprinkle the herbs over them, season with pepper, cover, and refrigerate for at least 1 hour.

FOR THE BERRY SAUCE, combine the berries, water, shallots, vinegar, crème de cassis (if using), and sugar in a medium-sized, heavy saucepan. Bring just to a boil; reduce the heat and simmer, stirring often, until the mixture is well blended and thick, 12 to 15 minutes. Season to taste with salt and pepper. If you prefer a very smooth sauce, purée it in a food processor and pass through a sieve back into the pan. Keep warm.

PREHEAT THE OVEN to 450°F. Lightly grease a baking sheet.

PUT THE FLOUR in a shallow dish and season liberally with salt and pepper. In another shallow dish, lightly beat the egg and milk. Put the ground hazelnuts in a third dish.

DIP A CHICKEN BREAST in the flour to coat, patting to remove excess flour. Dip the breast in the beaten egg, allow excess to drip off, then coat the breast evenly with the hazelnuts. Set the breast on the baking sheet and repeat with the remaining chicken breasts.

BAKE THE CHICKEN until cooked through, 12 to 15 minutes. Arrange each breast on an individual plate, drizzle some of the berry sauce over and around it, and serve immediately.

MAKES 4 SERVINGS

forest chicken

SOL DUC HOT SPRINGS ◆ PORT ANGELES, WASHINGTON

Sol Duc's former chef Mike Rogers featured this seductive recipe each fall, when local apples and wild mushrooms are abundant. Apricot-scented chanterelles are the chef's favorite, but morels, shiitakes, oyster mushrooms, or portobellos can all be used. Columbia Winery's smoky, earthy Red Willow Vineyard Syrah marries exceptionally well with this woodsy dish.

½ cup flour
Salt and freshly ground black pepper
4 bone-in chicken breasts (about 8 ounces each)
¼ cup olive oil
2 teaspoons chopped garlic
2 teaspoons minced shallot
8 ounces wild mushrooms, cleaned, trimmed, and sliced
½ cup veal stock or chicken stock
⅓ cup diced tart apple, such as Granny Smith or Gravenstein
¼ cup chopped walnuts
2 tablespoons dry sherry
2 tablespoons dry white wine
2 teaspoons minced tarragon
1 teaspoon minced thyme

PREHEAT THE OVEN to 350°F.

SEASON THE FLOUR with a generous pinch each of salt and pepper. Dust the chicken with the seasoned flour, patting to remove excess. In a large skillet, heat the oil over medium-high heat. Add the chicken and sauté until golden brown, 3 to 4 minutes on each side. Remove the chicken from the pan and set it in a shallow baking dish. Bake the chicken until it is no longer pink in the center of the thickest part, 15 to 20 minutes.

PREPARE THE SAUCE while the chicken is baking. Pour off all but about 1 table-spoon of the oil from the pan the chicken was cooked in, and reheat the pan over medium-high heat. Add the garlic and shallot and sauté for 1 minute. Add the

mushrooms and cook until just tender, about 3 minutes. Add the stock, apple, walnuts, sherry, wine, tarragon, and thyme. Cook, stirring occasionally, until reduced
by about half. Taste the sauce for seasoning, adding salt and pepper to taste.

ARRANGE THE CHICKEN BREASTS on individual plates, pour the sauce over them,
and serve immediately.

MAKES 4 SERVINGS

basic chicken stock

*Use whole chicken or meaty chicken parts for making stock, then take advantage of the cooked
meat for making chicken salad, pasta dishes, or other favorite recipes that use cooked chicken meat.*

2 to 3 pounds chicken backs, necks, or other portions, well rinsed
2 onions, quartered
2 large carrots, coarsely chopped
2 stalks celery, coarsely chopped
Bouquet garni of 3 parsley stems, 2 thyme sprigs, and 1 bay leaf, tied
   together with string
1 teaspoon black peppercorns
12 cups water, plus more if needed

PUT THE CHICKEN PARTS in a stockpot with the onions, carrots, celery, bouquet garni,
and peppercorns. Add water to cover, and bring just to a boil. Reduce the heat and simmer,
uncovered, until the stock is well flavored, about 2 hours. (If you are planning to use the meat
from the chicken, simmer the stock only 45 to 50 minutes and let the chicken cool in the
stock.) If necessary, add more hot water to the pot as it simmers so that the bones are always
covered. Use a large spoon to skim off scum that rises to the top.

STRAIN THE STOCK through a fine sieve or a colander lined with cheesecloth, discarding the
solids. Let cool, then skim off fat that rises to the surface. Chill and use within a few days, or
freeze for up to 1 month.

Makes about 8 cups

herbal tea–smoked chicken breast

THE SUTTON PLACE HOTEL ✦ VANCOUVER, BRITISH COLUMBIA

Infused with the smoky essence of herbal tea leaves, these grilled chicken breasts are napped with a fruity blueberry sauce. Sutton Place uses their own house blend herbal tea, but any herbal tea blend works well. The sauce gets body from demi-glace, a rich, concentrated stock that some stores sell in small disks. You may prefer to use a good chicken stock, but reduce it by half before adding the blueberries.

> 4 bone-in chicken breasts (about 8 ounces each), preferably grain-fed
> 1 tablespoon coarse salt
> 2 ounces herbal tea leaves (about 1½ cups)
> ½ cup unsalted butter
> 1 shallot, minced
> ¼ cup dry red wine
> 1 cup demi-glace or reduced chicken stock
> 1 cup fresh blueberries
> Salt and freshly ground black pepper

PUT THE CHICKEN in a shallow dish, sprinkle the coarse salt over it, and marinate in the refrigerator for 2 hours. Rinse off the salt and pat dry with paper towels.

PREHEAT AN OUTDOOR GRILL with a moderate fire. Soak the tea leaves in a bowl of warm tap water for 30 minutes. When the coals are hot, drain the tea leaves well and sprinkle them over the coals. Set the chicken on the grate, cover the grill, and smoke the chicken, without turning, until it is just cooked through, 20 to 30 minutes.

WHILE THE CHICKEN IS SMOKING, prepare the sauce. Heat 2 tablespoons of the butter in a medium saucepan until melted (chill the remaining butter). Add the shallot and cook over medium heat until softened, 2 to 3 minutes. Add the wine, bring to a boil, and boil until reduced by about half. Add the demi-glace and blueberries and simmer gently for 15 minutes. Cut the remaining butter into chunks, add it to the sauce, and stir so the butter melts gently into the sauce without separating. Season to taste with salt and pepper.

SET A CHICKEN BREAST on each individual plate and drizzle the sauce over and around it. Serve immediately.

MAKES 4 SERVINGS

rotini with seared quail breast, porcini mushrooms, and sage

CINCIN • VANCOUVER, BRITISH COLUMBIA

The integrity of this wintry pasta dish depends on the flavor of dried porcini mushrooms, which are much more flavorful than fresh ones.

1 to 2 ounces dried porcini mushrooms
½ cup hot water (more if needed)
12 ounces dried rotini pasta
2 tablespoons vegetable oil
8 whole, boned quail breasts
¼ cup minced shallot or onion
1 tablespoon minced garlic
1 cup quail stock (using the remaining portions of quail) or chicken stock
3 tablespoons minced sage
Pinch dried red pepper flakes
1 tablespoon unsalted butter, chilled
Salt and freshly ground black pepper
¼ cup grated Parmesan or Romano cheese

PUT THE MUSHROOMS in a small bowl, cover with the hot water, and soak to soften.

BRING A LARGE PAN of lightly salted water to a boil, add the pasta, and simmer until al dente, 7 to 10 minutes. Drain well, toss in 1 tablespoon of the oil, and set aside.

HEAT THE REMAINING 1 tablespoon of oil in a large, heavy skillet over medium-high heat. When hot, add the quail breasts and sear until nicely browned on each side but still rare, 1 to 2 minutes on each side. Set aside. Add the shallot and garlic to the skillet and cook over medium heat until just tender and fragrant, 2 to 3 minutes.

MEANWHILE, drain the mushrooms, reserving the liquid. Coarsely chop the mushrooms and add them to the skillet with their liquid. Bring to a boil and boil until the liquid is reduced to about 2 tablespoons. Add the stock and boil until reduced by about half. Add the quail breasts with the sage and red pepper flakes. Cook gently, stirring, until the quail is heated through, 2 to 3 minutes. Remove the skillet from the heat and add the butter, stirring until melted. Add the pasta and salt and pepper to taste, tossing to mix well.

DIVIDE THE PASTA among 4 individual plates, with 2 quail breasts on each plate. Sprinkle the grated cheese over all and serve immediately.

MAKES 4 SERVINGS

wild northwest mushrooms

With its mild, damp climate and rich woodland soils, the Pacific Northwest is a mushroom collector's paradise. The region is also home to two species of truffles—the Oregon white truffle and the Oregon black truffle. The following mushrooms grow wild in the Northwest; they are also commonly available in local markets. Because some wild mushrooms are highly toxic, you should consult an expert if you don't know how to identify them, or purchase them from a reputable market.

OYSTER MUSHROOM: *Pale-gray to beige, oyster mushrooms, with their frilly, oyster shell–shaped caps, have a delicate woodsy flavor with a hint of anise.*

BOLETUS: *Also known as porcini or cèpes, these golden-brown members of the Boletus edulis species are thick and meaty, with deep, intense flavor. They have bulbous stems and big, round caps that can stretch 8 inches across. Boletus are often sold dried.*

CHANTERELLE: *Wild golden chanterelles, with their delicate apricot scent and sweet, earthy flavor, are a favorite with Northwest cooks. Shaped like an umbrella that's been folded inside-out, chanterelles are harvested wild in the spring and fall. White and black chanterelles also grow wild in the Northwest, and the black chanterelle is cultivated locally on a small scale.*

MOREL: *Sweet and earthy, with a delicious caramel flavor when sautéed, morels are harvested wild each spring. They are frequently sold dried. Brown and shaped like pine cones, morels have a chambered outer flesh that resembles sponge or coral.*

MATSUTAKE: *Highly favored in Asian cooking, matsutake mushrooms have a pungent, spicy aroma similar to horseradish. They grow beneath Northwest pine trees and are harvested in the fall. These brown-gilled mushrooms have a cream- to beige-colored, 3- to 5-inch cap and stem.*

oil-poached rabbit legs with green goddess dressing

SITKA & SPRUCE ✦ SEATTLE, WASHINGTON

This is a wonderful way to cook rabbit that does not overwhelm the already delicate flavor of the animal. Owner and chef Matthew Dillion recommends asking your butcher to carve the fore and hind legs from two whole rabbits and using the remaining parts for other recipes. Note that preparation must begin the night before.

8 fore or hind rabbit legs
Salt for coating
1 to 2 cups extra-virgin olive oil
4 fresh bay leaves
3 sprigs fresh thyme
1 head garlic split widthwise
1 shallot, peeled and halved
1 lemon, quartered
2 teaspoons salt
1 tablespoon whole black peppercorns

Green Goddess Dressing

¾ cup lightly packed tarragon leaves
¾ cup lightly packed mint leaves
¼ cup lightly packed chives
¼ cup lightly packed parsley leaves
¼ cup lightly packed basil leaves
6 anchovy fillets
Zest of 1 lemon
Freshly squeezed juice of 2 lemons, plus more to taste
1 medium shallot, peeled and quartered
1 clove garlic, peeled
¾ cup whole-milk yogurt
6 tablespoons extra-virgin olive oil
Salt and freshly ground black pepper

THE NIGHT BEFORE, salt the rabbit legs thoroughly and place on a wire rack over a plate or tray. Cover and keep refrigerated.

TO MAKE THE DRESSING, put the tarragon, mint, chives, parsley, basil, anchovies, lemon zest and juice, shallot, garlic, and yogurt in a food processor with a blade attachment, or put in a large bowl and use a hand-held immersion blender. Purée until smooth and bright green, scraping the sides of the container as needed. With the machine or blender running, slowly add the olive oil. You should have a bright green, creamy dressing. Season with salt, pepper, and additional lemon juice to taste.

PREHEAT THE OVEN to 275°F.

IN A LARGE OVENPROOF CASSEROLE or baking pan large enough to fit all the rabbit legs, put first the larger hind legs, then the smaller ones on top. Fill with enough olive oil to cover the meat by 1 inch. Add the bay leaves, thyme, garlic, shallot, lemon, salt, and peppercorns.

BRING TO A SIMMER over medium-high heat, then cover and transfer to the oven. Cook for 1 hour, then check the smaller legs for tenderness. When the meat easily pulls away from the bone, they are done. Remove the smaller legs from the pot and place them on a plate to rest, returning the pan with the larger legs to the oven. Cook until the larger legs are tender, which may take up to an additional 30 minutes.

STRAIN THE OIL and pan juices through a mesh strainer into a tall clear container and let settle until the oil and juices separate, about 20 minutes. Return the rabbit legs to the pan. Carefully ladle out the oil and pour it over the rabbit legs. Return the legs to the stovetop and heat slowly until ready to serve.

PUT THE RESERVED PAN JUICES in a saucepan over medium heat until warm. Season to taste with salt and pepper.

TO SERVE, carefully lift the rabbit legs from the pan and place on a serving platter. Drizzle with the warm, seasoned pan juices and a squeeze of lemon. Serve with the green goddess dressing alongside.

MAKES 4 SERVINGS WITH 2 CUPS OF DRESSING

roasted rabbit with basque txakoli wine sauce

THE HARVEST VINE ◆ SEATTLE, WASHINGTON

Txakoli (pronounced "chac-o-lee") is a slightly sparkling, bright white wine produced in the Basque region of Spain that brings out the rich flavors of the rabbit in this dish. If you can't find the traditional wine, you can substitute a semi-sparkling variety. Be careful not to overroast this dish; rabbit is a lean meat that can easily become dry.

2 large yellow onions, cut into ¼-inch slices
1 whole rabbit, cleaned, with liver and kidneys reserved
Salt
2 tablespoons minced garlic
1 tablespoon minced flat-leaf (Italian) parsley
5 garlic cloves, peeled
6 small red potatoes, halved
½ cup olive oil
2 tablespoons unsalted butter
¼ cup flour
2 cups txakoli wine
1 tablespoon black peppercorns, freshly crushed
1 cup rabbit stock or chicken stock

PREHEAT THE OVEN to 400°F.

LINE THE BOTTOM of a roasting pan with the onion slices. Split the rabbit wide open and place it on the onion slices, belly up. Sprinkle with salt, half of the minced garlic, and half of the parsley. Put the garlic cloves, liver, kidneys, and potatoes around the rabbit. Drizzle ¼ cup of the oil over the entire contents of the pan. Roast in the oven for 30 minutes.

REMOVE THE PAN from the oven and turn the rabbit over. Sprinkle with more salt and the remaining garlic, parsley, and oil. Return the pan to the oven and roast until golden, about 30 minutes.

AFTER ROASTING, remove the rabbit body and the potatoes from the pan. Cut the rabbit into quarters and arrange on a platter with the potatoes. Cover with foil and keep warm.

MEANWHILE, place the roasting pan on top of the stove over medium-high heat. Add the butter and caramelize the onions, kidneys, and liver until dark brown, 8 to 10 minutes. Add the flour, mixing well. Deglaze the pan with the wine. Season to taste with salt and add the crushed peppercorns. Add the stock and cook, stirring, for 15 minutes or until reduced by a quarter. Transfer to a food processor or food mill and purée. Adjust the seasoning if needed. Strain through a colander, then drizzle over the platter of rabbit. Serve immediately.

MAKES 6 SERVINGS

cranberry pot roast

TOKELAND HOTEL & RESTAURANT ◆ TOKELAND, WASHINGTON

Some of the Northwest's most prized cranberry bogs are just a skipping-stone's-throw away from the Tokeland Hotel near Willapa Bay, so this variation on pot roast is a natural. When fresh berries aren't available, look for frozen or dried cranberries, or use 1 cup canned whole berries. Mashed potatoes and a fresh, fruity pinot noir from Montinore Vineyards complete this meal.

1 cup flour
1 teaspoon salt
½ teaspoon freshly ground black pepper
1 rump or bottom round beef roast, 5 to 6 pounds
Vegetable oil
1 cup dry white wine or water
1 stick cinnamon, broken into 2 or 3 pieces
10 whole cloves
2 cups whole cranberries
1 cup water
½ cup sugar

Gravy
¼ cup cornstarch
½ cup dry red wine
2 cups beef stock (see page 118)
Salt and freshly ground black pepper

PREHEAT THE OVEN to 350°F.

COMBINE THE FLOUR, salt, and pepper and thoroughly coat the roast in the seasoned flour. Over medium-high heat, heat about ¼ inch of oil in the bottom of a heavy Dutch oven or other heavy pan large enough to hold the roast. Add the roast and brown well on all sides. Add the wine, cinnamon stick, and cloves. Cover the pan and roast in the oven until the meat is quite tender, 3 to 3½ hours.

COOK THE CRANBERRIES while the meat is roasting. In a small pan, combine the cranberries, water, and sugar and simmer, stirring often, just until the sugar has dissolved and the berries begin to burst. Set aside.

WHEN THE ROAST IS TENDER, remove the pan from the oven and carefully ladle out and reserve all but about ½ inch of the pan drippings. Pour the cranberries and their liquid over the roast and return it to the oven, uncovered, for about 30 minutes.

MAKE THE GRAVY while the roast is finishing. Put the reserved pan drippings in a small saucepan. In a small bowl, stir together the cornstarch and wine. Add this mixture and the beef stock to the saucepan. Cook over medium heat, stirring constantly, just until the sauce thickens. Season to taste with salt and pepper.

TRANSFER THE ROAST to a carving board and cut into thick slices. Arrange the slices on a serving platter and spoon the cranberries and remaining pan drippings over. Serve immediately, passing the gravy separately.

MAKES 8 TO 10 SERVINGS

basic beef or veal stock

Ask your butcher to cut large bones into smaller pieces; they shouldn't weigh much over 1 pound each. Because stocks are often reduced to concentrate the flavor in recipes, it is best not to use salt when making stock. Season as needed when the stock is added to the recipe. For a light-colored stock, simply simmer (don't roast) the bones and vegetables. For a richer-flavored stock, boil the strained stock until reduced by about one-quarter.

> 4 pounds beef or veal bones
> 2 onions, quartered
> 2 large carrots, coarsely chopped
> 2 stalks celery, coarsely chopped
> Bouquet garni of 3 parsley stems, 2 thyme sprigs, and 1 bay leaf, tied
>   together with string
> 1 teaspoon black peppercorns
> 12 cups water, plus more if needed

PREHEAT THE OVEN to 425°F.

PUT THE BONES in a large roasting pan and scatter the onions, carrots, and celery around them. Roast until the bones are well browned, about 30 minutes. Stir occasionally so the bones brown evenly.

TRANSFER THE BONES and vegetables to a stockpot; add the bouquet garni and peppercorns. Add cold water to cover, bring to a boil, then lower the heat and simmer, uncovered, until the stock is brown and richly flavored, 3 to 4 hours. If necessary, add more hot water to the pot as it simmers so that the bones are always covered. Use a large spoon to skim off scum that rises to the top.

LIFT THE BONES from the stock with tongs and discard them. Strain the stock through a fine sieve or a colander lined with cheesecloth, discarding the solids. Let cool, then skim off fat that rises to the surface. Chill and use within a few days, or freeze for up to 1 month.

Makes about 8 cups

caretto d'agnello

Rich and robustly flavored, this delicious rack of lamb for two is worthy of a special Northwest red wine, such as a big, powerful D2 from Washington's DeLille Cellars. Note that the rack of lamb needs to marinate for one to two days.

1 rack of lamb, trimmed (about 8 ribs, 1½ pounds total)

Marinade
¼ cup chopped garlic
2 tablespoons chopped rosemary
2 tablespoons chopped oregano
1 tablespoon sea salt
2 large lemons, halved
1½ cups olive oil

Red Wine Sauce
1 tablespoon red wine vinegar
2 cups red wine
1 cup beef or veal stock (see page 118)
½ cup stewed or chopped fresh tomatoes
Pinch chopped rosemary
Pinch chopped garlic
2 tablespoons unsalted butter
Salt and freshly ground black pepper

FOR THE MARINADE, combine the garlic, rosemary, oregano, salt, lemon halves (lightly squeezed to release a little juice), and olive oil in a shallow pan. Add the lamb and rub all over with the marinade. Cover and let marinate in the refrigerator for 1 to 2 days, turning the rack a few times.

PREHEAT THE OVEN to 450°F.

HEAT A LARGE SAUTÉ PAN or skillet over medium-high heat. Remove the lamb from the marinade, put it in the pan, and brown it quickly on all sides. Transfer to a roasting pan and bake for 10 to 15 minutes for medium rare.

PREPARE THE SAUCE while the lamb is roasting. Discard all but 1 tablespoon of drippings from the sauté pan and reheat the pan. Add the vinegar and stir to deglaze the pan. Add the wine, stock, tomatoes, rosemary, and garlic, bring to a boil, and boil until reduced to about ¾ cup. Remove the pan from the heat, add the butter, and stir to gently melt it into the sauce. Season to taste with salt and pepper.

REMOVE THE LAMB from the oven and let it sit for a few minutes. Carve the rack into chops and serve with the sauce.

MAKES 2 SERVINGS

northwest lamb

No matter where lamb is raised in the pristine farmlands of the Pacific Northwest—whether on Salt Spring Island, in British Columbia, or in Ellensburg, Washington—its exceptionally mild, sweet flavor blends wonderfully with woodsy mushrooms, earthy root vegetables, toasted nuts, fruity olive oil, and savory herbs like garlic and rosemary.

To be designated as lamb, meat must come from an animal that is less than one year old. Once a seasonal item, lamb is now available year-round, in the form of leg of lamb, chops, racks, the sirloin leg steak (great for grilling), and top round roast (which can be sliced into medallions or steaks or roasted whole). Thanks to standards instituted in the lamb industry in 1990, consumers are assured of mild-flavored, lean, tender meat.

Judge freshness in lamb by the firmness of the legs, which should be thick and plump. Fat should be firm and white or creamy in color. Flesh should be firm, fine grained, and smooth and velvety to the touch. Meat should be light pink in color and should smell sweet and herbaceous.

roasted fallow venison wrapped in applewood-smoked bacon

THE HEATHMAN HOTEL ◆ PORTLAND, OREGON

Chef Philippe Boulot serves these tender medallions of venison alternating with slices of acorn squash that have been sautéed in butter, brown sugar, and whiskey. Boulot deep-fries the sage leaf garnish that accompanies the venison by simply dropping clean, dry leaves into a small pan of hot oil and removing them when they're lightly browned and fragrant. Balance the earthy intensity of this flavorful dish with a cabernet sauvignon from Washington's Columbia Valley.

¼ cup unsalted butter
½ cup flour

✖

1½ pounds venison tenderloin, trimmed of silver skin
¾ pound applewood-smoked bacon or other smoked bacon, thinly sliced
Sage leaves, for garnish

Huckleberry Grand Veneur Sauce
¼ cup unsalted butter
½ cup minced shallots
⅓ cup huckleberry jam
1 bottle pinot noir
⅓ cup huckleberries (fresh or frozen)

PREHEAT THE OVEN to 450°F.

FIRST MAKE A ROUX for the sauce. In a small saucepan, melt the butter. Add the flour and cook over low heat for 6 minutes, stirring constantly. Set aside to cool.

WRAP THE VENISON TENDERLOIN in bacon, slightly overlapping the slices; the ends do not need to be wrapped. Tie the bacon-wrapped loin with kitchen string, securing it well.

HEAT A HEAVY, OVENPROOF SAUTÉ PAN or skillet over high heat and sear the venison well on all sides, 4 to 5 minutes in all. Transfer the skillet to the oven and reduce the temperature immediately to 350°F. Roast the venison to the desired doneness, about 12 minutes for medium rare (130°F internal temperature), 15 minutes for medium (140°F).

MAKE THE SAUCE while the venison is roasting. Heat the butter in a large skillet, add the shallots, and cook over medium-high heat until they begin to soften, 1 to 2 minutes. Stir in the huckleberry jam and continue cooking until it begins to bubble and is slightly caramelized, 2 to 3 minutes. Slowly pour in the pinot noir, bring to a boil, and boil until reduced by half, 12 to 15 minutes.

WHEN THE WINE has reduced, stir in the huckleberries. Add the roux, about a tablespoon at a time, stirring well to incorporate each addition, until the sauce has a thick but still pourable consistency. Keep warm over very low heat.

REMOVE THE VENISON ROAST from the oven, discard the kitchen string, and let the roast sit for a few minutes before carving. To serve, cut the roast into medallions about 1 inch thick. Arrange them around the center of the individual plates, spoon the sauce over them, garnish with sage leaves, and serve immediately.

MAKES 4 SERVINGS

venison

Venison contains only 3 to 5 percent fat (compared to beef at 20 percent fat) and almost no cholesterol. Some of the freshest, mildest-tasting venison comes from fallow deer, which have been bred in captivity for more than five thousand years. Fallow deer is currently raised on a small scale throughout the Northwest, and the meat is available at specialty butcher shops.

Besides being milder in flavor than wild venison, farm-raised fallow deer are much more tender. Recipes for wild venison often call for acidic marinades and a long, slow cooking process to tame the wild flavor and tenderize the meat. With farm-raised fallow deer, these steps are unnecessary. Cuts can be treated much like good-quality cuts of lean beef.

parisienne gnocchi with snails and garlic

LE PIGEON ✦ PORTLAND, OREGON

Parisienne gnocchi—made without potato starch—are more akin to pâte à choux *dough, rather than the Italian gnocchi dough. At Le Pigeon, chef Gabriel Rucker makes a marrow butter to give the gnocchi a deeper, richer flavor. However, the dish is delicious made with regular butter as well.*

Marrow Butter (optional)
2 or 3 marrow bones
3 tablespoons softened unsalted butter

✕

3 cups loosely packed flat-leaf (Italian) parsley, leaves only
3 eggs
6 tablespoons marrow butter (recipe above) or unsalted butter
Salt and freshly ground black pepper
1 cup flour
2 tablespoons unsalted butter
One 6-ounce can high-quality snails, drained
3 cloves chopped garlic
Freshly squeezed juice of 1 lemon
High-quality flake sea salt, such as Fleur de Sel
1 tablespoon chopped flat-leaf (Italian) parsley

TO MAKE THE MARROW BUTTER, preheat the oven to 400°F and roast the marrow bones until the marrow starts to pull away from the bones, about 15 minutes. Scoop out the marrow and allow it to cool to room temperature. Whip together 3 table-spoons of the bone marrow with the unsalted butter until evenly incorporated.

TO MAKE THE GNOCCHI, bring a pot of water to a boil. Add the 3 cups of parsley. After 10 seconds in the water, drain and plunge the parsley into a bowl of ice water. When the parsley is cold, drain and squeeze dry. Put it in a blender with the eggs, and purée until the mixture is a smooth, light green.

COMBINE 1½ CUPS WATER, marrow butter or regular butter, salt, and pepper in a heavy-bottomed saucepan and bring to a boil. Reduce the heat to medium. Add the flour all at once, and stir rapidly with a wooden spoon until the dough pulls away from the sides and bottom of the pan. Continue to stir until the dough begins to steam and release an aroma of cooked flour.

TRANSFER THE DOUGH to the bowl of a mixer and let cool for 5 minutes. Using the paddle attachment, work the dough for about 2 minutes. Slowly add the egg mixture, one-sixth at a time, incorporating each portion fully before adding the next.

BRING A LARGE POT of salted water to a boil and oil a baking sheet.

TRANSFER THE GNOCCHI DOUGH to a pastry bag fitted with a medium (⅝-inch) tip. Turn the water down to a simmer. Holding the bag over the side of the pot with one hand and a small knife in the other, squeeze out segments of about 1 inch and slice so each drops into the pot. The gnocchi will sink to the bottom. When they rise to the top, 1 to 2 minutes, they are done. Use a slotted spoon to remove the cooked gnocchi and transfer to the baking sheet.

JUST BEFORE SERVING, heat the 2 tablespoons butter in a large sauté pan over medium-high heat. Add the gnocchi and swirl for 1 to 2 minutes to warm them. Add the snails and garlic. When the garlic has softened, add the lemon juice to halt the cooking. Divide among 6 bowls and top with sea salt and parsley.

MAKES 6 SERVINGS

salmon with split peas, spinach, and bacon in a mussel broth

THE INN AT LANGLEY ◦ LANGLEY, WASHINGTON

The Inn at Langley has always celebrated the charm of Northwestern islands. General manager and chef Matt Costello brings that spirit to the dinner table with dishes that include ingredients from the Inn's own gardens, local farmers markets, and even foraged finds from hiking trails around the island. And of course, fresh seafood always plays a big role in the Inn's tasting menu. Costello recommends pairing this dish with another local find, the '02 DeLille Cellars Chaleur Estate Blanc.

1 cup dried yellow split peas
4 tablespoons unsalted butter
Freshly squeezed juice of 2 lemons
Salt and freshly ground black pepper
4 wild salmon fillets, 4 to 5 ounces each
1 tablespoon olive oil
1 shallot, sliced
¼ cup finely diced cooked bacon
2 pounds Penn Cove mussels
1 cup fruity white wine, such as Sauvignon Blanc
4 tablespoons crème fraîche
High-quality, extra-virgin olive oil, for garnish

Sautéed Spinach
4 cups loosely packed fresh baby spinach, cleaned
1 tablespoon unsalted butter
1 tablespoon minced shallot
Freshly squeezed juice of 1 lemon
Salt and freshly ground black pepper

PREHEAT THE OVEN to 325°F.

COOK THE PEAS in 3 cups of water over medium heat until al dente, about 25 minutes. Drain the peas and lightly rinse. Place the peas in a heavy-bottomed pot over low heat. Stir in 2 tablespoons of the butter and the juice of 1 lemon, and season with salt and pepper. Keep the peas warm while preparing the rest of the dish.

RINSE THE SALMON FILLETS and pat dry with a paper towel. Season with salt and pepper.

HEAT A SAUTÉ PAN large enough to hold 2 of the salmon fillets over medium-high heat. Add the olive oil and the fillets, and sear on the flesh side. Remove the fillets from the pan and place in a baking pan, seared side up. Repeat with the remaining 2 fillets. Bake until the fish is opaque, 5 to 7 minutes. Remove from the oven and keep warm.

IN A SEPARATE SAUTÉ PAN, sauté the shallot with the bacon over medium-high heat until the shallot is soft and translucent. Add the mussels and deglaze the pan with the wine. When the mussels open (2 to 5 minutes), pour off the broth into a bowl. Discard any that do not open. Cover to keep the mussels warm.

WHISK THE REMAINING 2 tablespoons of butter into the mussel broth and reduce slightly. Add the remaining juice of 1 lemon and set aside.

TO MAKE THE SAUTÉED SPINACH, sauté the spinach in the butter and season with the minced shallot, lemon juice, salt, and pepper.

TO SERVE, divide the warm peas among 4 serving bowls and place a salmon fillet on each. Top the salmon with the spinach and a dollop of crème fraîche. Top with three of the mussels in their shells. Tuck a few more mussels around the salmon. Pour the broth around the fillet, and drizzle the dish with a bit of olive oil. Serve immediately.

MAKES 4 SERVINGS

wild salmon of the pacific northwest

KING, CHINOOK, TYEE, OR BLACKMOUTH: This is the largest and rarest of the Pacific species, averaging 15 to 40 pounds, with some specimens weighing up to 100 pounds. Kings, whose flesh color ranges from a rich "salmon" shade to almost white, are highly prized for their fat content, which imparts complex flavor and rich texture. Kings are mainly available from May to September. The fattest king salmon are Columbia River chinooks, Alaskan Yukon kings, and Copper River kings.

COHO, OR SILVER: Average market size for the coho salmon is 5 to 10 pounds, although some can grow to over 20 pounds. Like the meat of a king salmon, coho meat, which ranges in color from rich orange-red to pale pink, forms large flakes when cooked. Cohos are firm fleshed and extremely flavorful. Their season runs from July through September.

SOCKEYE, RED, OR BLUEBACK: The deep-red flesh of sockeye is tightly grained, with a robust flavor. These are the second fattiest of the Pacific salmon, generally weighing 5 to 7 pounds. They are available from late May through July. Look for fish from British Columbia's Fraser River and Alaska's Cooper River.

CHUM, KETA, DOG, OR FALL: Chum meat is less fatty than other salmon and usually paler in color; some chums, however, have a good reddish-orange color and earthy flavor. These fish are available from July through October.

PINK, OR HUMPIE: Pinks are the smallest and most abundant of the Pacific salmon. The meat, as the name suggests, is usually pink in color and delicately flavored. Because of their small size, pinks are excellent for grilling whole; however, most of the pink harvest goes into cans.

roasted red king salmon with pesto crust and spinach and tomato napoleons

THE HEATHMAN HOTEL ◦ PORTLAND, OREGON

For a special occasion, try this fragrant pesto-encrusted king salmon, served with a flavorful napoleon made with layers of oven-dried beefsteak tomatoes and fresh spinach. Note that the tomatoes need to dry in the oven for at least 2 hours, so plan ahead; they can be prepared one day in advance and stored in an airtight container.

4 salmon fillet pieces (7 to 8 ounces each), bones removed

Spinach and Tomato Napoleons

½ teaspoon ground coriander

½ teaspoon ground cumin

½ teaspoon freshly ground black pepper

½ teaspoon salt

½ teaspoon minced garlic

2 large, ripe beefsteak tomatoes, cored and cut into ¼-inch slices

¼ cup olive oil

1 shallot, minced

1½ pounds spinach, tough stems removed (about 2 bunches)

Salt and freshly ground black pepper

Pesto Crust

¼ cup coarsely chopped basil

¼ cup bread crumbs

2 tablespoons pine nuts

2 tablespoons grated Parmesan cheese

2 slices bacon, chopped

1 clove garlic

2 tablespoons olive oil

Red Onion Cilantro Relish

2 tablespoons olive oil

1 large or 2 small red onions, diced (about 2 cups)

½ teaspoon minced garlic

½ teaspoon minced ginger

¼ cup freshly squeezed lemon juice

1 tablespoon soy sauce

1 teaspoon red chile garlic paste (such as sambal oelek) or minced
    fresh chile

1 teaspoon drained capers

1 teaspoon thinly sliced green onion

1 teaspoon minced flat-leaf (Italian) parsley

1 teaspoon minced cilantro

PREHEAT THE OVEN to 200°F.

TO OVEN-DRY THE TOMATOES, stir together the coriander, cumin, pepper, salt, and garlic in a small bowl. Line a baking sheet with parchment paper or foil and sprinkle half of the seasonings over it. Arrange the tomato slices on the sheet, brush the tops with 2 tablespoons of the olive oil, and sprinkle the remaining seasonings over them. Dry in the oven until slightly wrinkled looking, 2 to 3 hours. Set aside on paper towels.

HEAT THE REMAINING 2 tablespoons olive oil in a large skillet, add the shallot, and sauté for 1 minute. Add the spinach and cook, stirring, until thoroughly wilted. Season to taste with salt and pepper and set aside.

FOR THE PESTO CRUST, combine the basil, bread crumbs, pine nuts, Parmesan, bacon, and garlic in a food processor and process until well mixed. With the machine running, slowly add the olive oil. Alternatively, mix the ingredients well with a fork, and then drizzle in the olive oil while continuing to stir, mixing until evenly moistened. Season to taste with salt and pepper.

FOR THE RELISH, heat the olive oil in a large skillet over medium-high heat. Add the red onion and cook, stirring, until the onion gives off some liquid and begins to soften, 3 to 4 minutes. Add the garlic and ginger and cook for 1 minute longer. Stir in the lemon juice and continue cooking until most of the liquid has evaporated, about 2 minutes. Stir in the soy sauce, chile garlic paste, capers, green onion, parsley, and cilantro. Taste the mixture for seasoning, transfer to a bowl, and refrigerate. (Cooling the relish quickly helps preserve the texture and color of the onions.)

PREHEAT THE OVEN to 400°F.

PRESS THE PESTO CRUST MIXTURE onto the flesh side of each salmon fillet piece, forming a crust about ⅛ inch thick. Heat a large, ovenproof, nonstick skillet until very hot, add the salmon, crust side down, and sear until nicely browned, 1 to 2 minutes. Flip the salmon crust side up, put it in the oven and bake until just opaque in the center, 5 to 8 minutes, depending on the thickness of the fillets.

ASSEMBLE THE SPINACH and tomato napoleons while the salmon is baking. On each of 4 plates, press 1 tablespoon of the spinach mixture into a small circle and set a tomato slice on top. Add another layer of spinach, and top with another tomato slice. Repeat once more, for a triple-layer napoleon.

SPOON SOME RED ONION RELISH onto each plate and set the pesto-crusted salmon on top. Serve immediately, passing any remaining relish separately.

MAKES 4 SERVINGS

buying fish 101

Selecting quality fish is no more difficult than choosing good-quality fruits or vegetables. It's simply a matter of using your senses. Look for fish that smell clean and fresh. The scales should be intact, and the bright, iridescent skin protected by a slippery, viscous coating. The body should be firm and elastic, bouncing back when you press it, and the eyes bright, round, and transparent.

It also helps to know how the fish was harvested, cleaned, and transported. Fish caught in gill nets are more likely to have bruised, spotted flesh than fish caught with a hook and line. Further bruising can occur while the fish are stored in the boat holds. Also, fish should be bled and gutted immediately after capture. Some fishers flash-freeze the fish aboard ship after cleaning them.

When buying a whole fish, check inside of it to make sure it's been properly cleaned. Look for bright-red gills. Avoid fish with "belly burns" (brown spots of deterioration), dark spots in the flesh, loss of scales, a fishy smell, or tears in the skin.

When buying fish fillets and steaks, look for shiny, translucent flesh with no fishy odor. Avoid any white fish that has pink bruise spots or that is gray or brown (which indicates aging). With fish that have tan or cream-colored flesh, such as tuna or shark, avoid any that have dark (blood) streaks.

If a fish is not chilled properly, the quality will deteriorate rapidly. Whole fish should be buried in ice, which will keep the temperature of the fish at 32°F. As the ice melts, it rinses away bacteria. Fillets should be wrapped and kept chilled at 32°F over ice; ice sitting on top of a fillet will seep into it. Freezing fish at home is not recommended. Most home freezers do not maintain cold enough temperatures to prevent ice crystals from damaging the fish.

herbed baked salmon on rock salt with late-summer tomato salad

WILDWOOD ✦ PORTLAND, OREGON

Slow-baking salmon on a bed of rock salt helps distribute the heat more evenly, ensuring moist texture and rich flavor. For a festive tomato salad, use yellow and red pear tomatoes, cherry tomatoes, and currant tomatoes.

1½ pounds salmon fillet, skin on, bones removed
1 tablespoon minced tarragon
1 tablespoon minced basil
1 tablespoon minced flat-leaf (Italian) parsley
1 tablespoon minced thyme
1 tablespoon fennel seeds, lightly crushed
Salt and freshly ground black pepper
3 cups rock salt or kosher salt, plus more if needed

Tomato Salad

1 pound mixed small tomatoes, halved
½ red onion, halved and sliced
3 cloves garlic, minced
½ cup lightly packed basil leaves
½ cup olive oil
2 tablespoons balsamic vinegar
Salt and freshly ground black pepper

PREHEAT THE OVEN to 325°F.

RUB THE SALMON with the tarragon, basil, parsley, thyme, and fennel seeds, distributing them evenly. Season lightly with salt and pepper. Cover a large baking sheet with foil and spread the rock salt over it.

SET THE SALMON FILLET, skin side down, on the bed of salt and bake it until the fish is just cooked through, 35 to 45 minutes.

PREPARE THE TOMATO SALAD while the salmon bakes. Combine the tomatoes, onion, garlic, and basil in a large bowl. Drizzle the oil and vinegar over the salad, toss gently to mix, and season to taste with salt and pepper. Let sit for at least 15 minutes before serving.

WHEN THE SALMON IS DONE, remove the pan from the oven and let sit for 5 minutes. Brush off excess salt, cut the fillet into 4 serving portions, and arrange on individual plates. Spoon the tomato salad alongside the salmon and serve.

MAKES 4 SERVINGS

salmon in the native tradition

Salmon played a central role in the lives and cultures of Northwest Native Americans. Many tribes believed that they and the salmon were descended from the same ancestors, and that salmon sacrificed themselves to benefit humankind. When a Chinook fisherman caught the season's first salmon, the fish was eaten ceremonially, and the heart was removed and thrown back to the sea to ensure new life.

The Native peoples still hold salmon celebrations each spring to honor the first salmon of the season. One of the oldest and largest salmon celebrations in the Northwest is the Celilo Wy-Am Salmon Feast and Pow Wow, held each April at the Celilo Village, just east of The Dalles on the Oregon side of the Columbia River. Before The Dalles Dam was built in 1957, Celilo Falls, one of the largest falls on the Columbia River, was a mecca for Indian fishermen, who gathered by the thousands each spring and fall to spear or net salmon.

In the traditional Native method of cooking salmon, the fish is held in a sturdy split pole with an interlacing web of cedar sticks. The pole is stuck in the ground near a slow-burning fire, one with glowing embers that emit a steady heat. (Northwest alder is the favored wood for cooking salmon.) The salmon cooks slowly, basting itself with its own oils while absorbing the fragrant smoke of the fire. Salmon cooked this way achieves a complexity of flavors and textures unattainable with any other method.

roasted steelhead with mint-hazelnut pesto and mashed potatoes with celery root and pear

RIVERPLACE HOTEL • PORTLAND, OREGON

This is comfort food, ideal for those wet, wintry days for which the Northwest is famous. The recipe combines three favorite Northwest ingredients: steelhead, hazelnuts, and mint.

Mint-Hazelnut Pesto

1 cup loosely packed spearmint leaves
5 cloves garlic
¼ cup pine nuts
¼ cup grated Parmesan cheese
½ cup olive oil
Salt and freshly ground black pepper
½ cup hazelnuts, toasted and coarsely chopped

Fresh Tomato Coulis

6 plum (Roma) tomatoes (about 1 pound), cored and quartered
2 tablespoons extra-virgin olive oil
Salt and freshly ground black pepper

Mashed Potatoes with Celery Root and Pear

1 pound russet potatoes, peeled and cut into 1-inch dice
1 pound celery root, peeled and cut into 1-inch dice
1 pound pears, preferably Bartlett or d'Anjou, peeled and cut into
   1-inch dice
½ cup milk
2 tablespoons unsalted butter
Salt and freshly ground black pepper

✕

2¼ pounds steelhead fillet, cut into 6 serving pieces
1 tablespoon vegetable oil

FOR THE PESTO, combine the spearmint, garlic, pine nuts, and Parmesan in a food processor and blend until very smooth. With the machine running, slowly pour in the olive oil. Season to taste with salt and pepper. Transfer the pesto to a bowl and stir in the chopped hazelnuts. Set aside.

FOR THE TOMATO COULIS, purée the tomatoes in a food processor or blender. Add the olive oil and continue processing until the coulis is thick and well mixed. Pass the mixture through a strainer to remove seeds and bits of skin. Season to taste with salt and pepper, put the coulis in a small saucepan, and gently warm over low heat.

FOR THE MASHED POTATOES, combine the potato and celery root in a large pan with just enough water to cover. Bring to a boil, lower the heat, and simmer until the potatoes are nearly tender, 12 to 15 minutes. Add the pears and simmer 5 minutes longer.

MEANWHILE, heat the milk with the butter in a small saucepan just until the butter has melted. Drain the potato mixture well and return it to the pan. Add the warm milk mixture and mash. (Do not thoroughly purée the mixture—a few lumps are desirable.) Season to taste with salt and pepper and cover the pan to keep warm.

PREHEAT THE OVEN to 375°F.

DRIZZLE THE STEELHEAD PIECES with the oil and rub it thoroughly over the fish. Heat a large, ovenproof skillet, preferably nonstick, over high heat. Add the fish pieces, skin side up, and sear for 1 to 2 minutes. (Don't disturb the fish for the first minute or it will stick.) Turn the fish and sear on the skin side for 1 to 2 minutes. Spread about 1 tablespoon of the pesto over each piece of fish, then transfer the skillet to the oven. Bake until the fish is nearly opaque, 7 to 10 minutes.

TO SERVE, spoon a generous dollop of mashed potatoes into the center of 6 individual plates. Drizzle some of the warm tomato coulis around the potatoes and set a portion of fish over the potatoes. Grind some pepper over the coulis and serve.

MAKES 6 SERVINGS

steelhead

Wild West Coast steelhead, or saltwater rainbow trout, are anadromous, meaning that they live in saltwater but spawn in freshwater rivers (like most salmon species). The flesh color ranges from ivory to brilliant red, depending on the fish's diet. Fish that consume large quantities of crayfish or shrimp will be more vibrantly colored. Steelhead meat is generally dark pink when cooked, similar to salmon, and is very flavorful.

Wild steelhead are usually larger than inland rainbow trout, and fish weighing 6 to 12 pounds are not uncommon. In the Northwest there are two wild steelhead runs, one during the summer months and the other in the winter, from December through April. Because just a tiny commercial harvest of wild steelhead is allowed in the Pacific Northwest, these fish can be difficult to find. It is illegal to sell wild steelhead in Oregon, but they can be caught there and sold outside the state. In Washington, Native American fishermen can catch and sell wild steelhead on a highly regulated basis.

black cod sake kasu

RAY'S BOATHOUSE ✦ SEATTLE, WASHINGTON

This exquisite sake kasu black cod is almost synonymous with Seattle's famed Ray's Boathouse. Sake kasu is a thick paste made from the lees, or leftovers, from the sake-fermenting process. It is available by the pound at Japanese specialty stores. Note that this preparation requires 48 hours to achieve its characteristic complex flavor, so plan ahead. To match the flavors of this complex dish, serve an equally complex wine, such as Ponzi Vineyards' Reserve Oregon pinot noir.

2 to 2½ pounds black cod fillet, skin on, bones removed, cut into 4 serving pieces

½ cup kosher or table salt, plus more if needed

6 ounces (¾ cup) sake kasu paste

⅓ cup sugar

¾ cup water

Fresh ginger, thinly sliced and blanched, or pickled ginger, for serving

SET THE BLACK COD PIECES skin side down in a shallow dish. Sprinkle a generous layer of salt over the fish, cover with plastic wrap, and refrigerate for 24 hours.

RINSE THE SALT from the fish and pat dry, then return the fish to the cleaned dish.

STIR TOGETHER the sake kasu paste and sugar in a small bowl until smooth. Slowly stir in the water. Pour the sake kasu mixture evenly over the fish, cover, and refrigerate for another 24 hours.

LIGHT THE COALS in an outdoor grill. When the coals are very hot, remove the black cod from the marinade, allowing the excess to drip off, and grill over the hot coals until nicely browned and just cooked through, about 5 minutes on each side. Transfer the fish to individual plates, top with fresh or pickled ginger slices, and serve.

MAKES 4 SERVINGS

flash-freezing: when frozen means fresh

Bruce Gore has been fishing the waters of Southeast Alaska for more than twenty-five years. During that time he has developed a unique process of flash-freezing just-caught salmon aboard ship. Gore's flash-freezing process has not only given him an edge on the competition, but it has also greatly influenced the quality of salmon available on the Northwest market.

"Most fish is frozen by default, because it's too old," explains Gore. "What we do is designate fish to be frozen from the beginning, when it's in its prime. Fish that is nonfrozen is often mistakenly labeled as 'fresh.' But the opposite of fresh isn't frozen—it's rotten."

The flash-freezing process starts aboard the fishing boat, where the salmon are caught with hook and line. Each fish is pulled to the side of the boat and stunned with a gaff hook, leaving the fish intact. Once the fish are aboard, they are live-bled, eviscerated, and flash frozen at −40°F, all within a matter of minutes.

Gore refers to this process as "stopping the biological clock." "The fish are frozen pre-rigor mortis," he explains, "so there is no enzymatic activity to degrade the product." Gore has each fish marked with a colored tag bearing his name and a number, enabling him to track when and where each fish was caught.

When Gore's salmon are thawed, they are so clean and brilliant, you'd swear they had just been pulled from the icy waters. Culinary luminaries, including Julia Child (who featured a Bruce Gore king salmon on one of her cooking shows), have selected Gore's frozen fish over nonfrozen in blind taste tests. In Japan, where his salmon are favored for sashimi, Gore's fish set the quality standard against which they judge all other salmon.

fillet of sole stuffed with shrimp and scallops

LA BERENGERIE ❋ GALIANO ISLAND, BRITISH COLUMBIA

Colorful seafood roll-ups of snowy white sole, stuffed with a speckled purée of Galiano Island shrimp and pink swimming (also known as singing) scallops, are contrasted by a vivid orange sauce made with roasted red peppers.

2 red bell peppers

2 tablespoons olive oil

1 medium onion, chopped

2 cloves garlic, minced

1 bay leaf

3 sprigs cilantro

1 cup white wine

1 pound pink swimming (singing) scallops in the shell, or 4 ounces
    bulk raw scallops

4 ounces medium shrimp, peeled and deveined

¼ cup pine nuts

¼ cup bread crumbs

2 tablespoons minced cilantro

2 tablespoons sour cream

Salt and freshly ground black pepper

4 sole fillets (about 4 ounces each)

¼ cup whipping cream

2 tablespoons capers, for garnish

ROAST THE RED PEPPERS over a gas flame or under the broiler, turning often, until evenly charred. Put the peppers in a paper or plastic bag, close the bag, and let sit until cool enough to handle. Peel away and discard the skin, then halve the peppers, discarding the cores and seeds. Set aside.

HEAT 1 TABLESPOON of the olive oil in a large saucepan. Add half the onion and half the garlic and cook over medium heat, stirring, until fragrant, 2 to 3 minutes. Add the bay leaf, cilantro sprigs, and wine. Bring just to a boil, add the scallops, cover the pan, and cook until the scallops have opened, 6 to 8 minutes. (If using bulk scallops, gently poach until just opaque, 3 to 5 minutes.) Remove the scallops and let cool for a few minutes. Strain the cooking liquid and reserve (you should have about ¾ cup).

TAKE THE SCALLOPS from their shells, removing the black part and the vein on the side. Put the scallops in a food processor or blender with the shrimp, pine nuts, bread crumbs, minced cilantro, sour cream, and half of 1 roasted red pepper. Process until just smooth, and season with a pinch each of salt and pepper.

PREHEAT THE OVEN to 350°F.

LAY THE SOLE FILLETS, smoother side up, on the work surface. Spread each fillet with about one-fourth of the stuffing and roll it up, beginning at the narrow end. Set the rolls, seam side down, in a lightly greased baking dish. Bake until opaque through (cut into 1 roll to test), about 20 minutes.

PREPARE THE SAUCE while the sole is baking. Heat the remaining 1 tablespoon olive oil in a medium saucepan. Add the remaining onion and garlic and cook over medium heat until fragrant, 2 to 3 minutes. Add the remaining roasted red peppers and the reserved scallop cooking liquid. Bring to a boil, reduce the heat, and simmer for 10 to 15 minutes. Let cool for about 10 minutes, then blend the mixture in a food processor or blender until smooth. Return the sauce to the pan and stir in the whipping cream, adding salt and pepper to taste. Keep warm over low heat.

SET A STUFFED SOLE FILLET on each of 4 individual plates, and spoon the sauce over and around them. Sprinkle the capers over the fillets and serve immediately.

MAKES 4 SERVINGS

sole and flounder

Early on, U.S. fishmongers figured out that if they called flounder "sole," it sold much better than the same fish marketed as flounder. So here in the Pacific Northwest, fish known as "sole" is actually flounder unless it's been imported; the only true soles (such as Dover and thickback) are found in seas from the Mediterranean to Denmark.

The three most common varieties of sole sold in the Northwest are petrale sole, a large Pacific flounder found from the Mexican border north to Alaska; rex sole, a small Pacific flounder found from southern California to the Bering Sea; and lemon sole, a winter flounder weighing more than three pounds. These delicate-tasting fish are interchangeable in recipes.

Flounder and sole, along with plaice, halibut, and turbot, are known as flatfish. These bottom dwellers are distinguished by having both eyes on top of their heads. Many have the ability to change color when threatened, allowing them to blend unnoticeably into sand or rock.

Fillets vary in color, from white to ivory to gray, depending on the species. The meat of most sole is thin and delicate and should be cooked very quickly. When done, the fish will turn white and opaque.

pescado rojo
(sole with red chile garlic salsa)

THE RIO CAFE • ASTORIA, OREGON

Chile lovers will relish this fiery salsa flavored with roasted chiles and lots of fresh garlic. The recipe is from the chef's family in Mexico. At The Rio Cafe, this dish is served with pinto beans, Mexican rice, and homemade corn tortillas. Any of our Northwest flounders will work nicely in this dish. Look for petrale sole, lemon sole, or rex sole.

Red Chile Garlic Salsa
½ cup dried whole red chiles (chiles de arbol)
¾ cup boiling water
¼ cup chopped onion
5 cloves garlic
1 tablespoon coarsely chopped cilantro
1½ teaspoons paprika
1½ teaspoons ground cayenne
1½ teaspoons dried red pepper flakes
½ teaspoon chili powder
½ teaspoon ground cumin
½ teaspoon salt
½ teaspoon freshly squeezed lemon juice

✖

1 cup flour
Salt and freshly ground black pepper
2 eggs
⅓ cup milk
2 cups finely ground cracker crumbs or bread crumbs
1½ pounds sole fillets
¼ cup vegetable oil, plus more if needed

FOR THE SALSA, put the whole chiles in a dry, heavy skillet over high heat. When hot, shake the pan so the chiles heat evenly; they should be about half blackened. Immediately put the chiles in a bowl, pour the boiling water over them, and set aside until lukewarm.

PUT THE CHILES and their soaking water in a food processor with the onion, garlic, cilantro, paprika, cayenne, red pepper flakes, chili powder, cumin, salt, and lemon juice. Process until well mixed but still slightly chunky. Alternatively, chop each of the ingredients finely, and mix together in a medium bowl. Set aside.

TO PREPARE THE FISH, put the flour in a large, shallow dish and season generously with salt and pepper. Beat the eggs with the milk in a shallow bowl. Put the cracker crumbs in another large, shallow dish. Lightly dust a large plate with flour.

DIP A SOLE FILLET in the seasoned flour, patting to remove the excess. Then dip it into the egg mixture to coat. Finally, thoroughly dredge the fillet in the cracker crumbs, patting to remove the excess. Set aside on the floured plate and repeat with the remaining fillets.

HEAT THE OIL in a large, heavy skillet over medium heat. Add the sole fillets and cook until golden brown, about 2 minutes. Turn the fillets, then drizzle about 1 teaspoon of the salsa over each fillet. Continue cooking until the sole is just cooked through, about 2 minutes longer, depending on the thickness of the fillets. Transfer the fillets to individual plates. Serve immediately, passing the extra salsa separately.

MAKES 4 SERVINGS

grilled crab and cheddar sandwich

TOKELAND HOTEL & RESTAURANT ✦ TOKELAND, WASHINGTON

Nothing showcases Northwest Dungeness crab better than simplicity. Here's a standout sandwich that needs nothing more than a crank of freshly ground black pepper.

2 cups crabmeat (about ¾ pound)
2 cups grated sharp cheddar cheese
4 to 5 tablespoons mayonnaise
8 slices sourdough bread
3 tablespoons unsalted butter, melted, plus more if needed

PICK OVER THE CRABMEAT to remove any bits of shell or cartilage.

COMBINE THE CRABMEAT and cheese in a large bowl and stir to mix. Add enough mayonnaise to hold the mixture together.

SPREAD THE CRAB MIXTURE on 4 slices of the bread and top with the remaining bread. Brush the tops with some of the melted butter. Heat a heavy skillet or griddle over medium heat. Add the sandwiches, buttered side down, and toast until browned, about 2 minutes. Brush the tops with more butter, turn the sandwiches, and continue toasting until the second side is browned and the cheese has melted, 2 to 3 minutes longer.

TRANSFER THE SANDWICHES to individual plates and serve, cut in half if desired.

MAKES 4 SERVINGS

spot prawns with baby chick-peas, meyer lemon, and herb coulis

TILTH ◦ SEATTLE, WASHINGTON

Spot prawns are one of the few "green" choices left when it comes to shrimp, because they are trap-caught rather than farmed. They are plentiful all along the west coast from California to Alaska. The prawns are caught in traps that resemble lobster and crab traps, from which fish can escape, and the shrimp are landed alive. Maria Hines, the chef-owner of Tilth and an advocate for organic meals, created the coulis of organic mint, cilantro, and parsley spooned on top of the prawns to accent the fresh flavors and textures. Note that the chick-peas need to soak overnight.

1 pound fresh spot prawns

Baby Chick-peas
¼ cups dried baby chick-peas
2 stalks celery
1 small yellow onion
1 medium carrot
2 bay leaves
½ teaspoon salt

Herb Coulis
1 bunch mint, leaves only
1 bunch cilantro, leaves only
1 bunch parsley, leaves only
3 cloves garlic, roasted
Freshly squeezed juice of ½ lemon
1 teaspoon kosher salt
½ teaspoon red pepper flakes
3 tablespoons extra-virgin olive oil

Beurre Fondue

1 cup unsalted butter
1 cup fresh heavy cream
1 lemon, zested and cut into segments
1 teaspoon kosher salt
Pinch ground white pepper

REMOVE THE SHELLS from the prawns.

SOAK THE BABY CHICK-PEAS overnight in a bowl of water to cover. When ready to cook them, drain and discard the water. Put 2 cups of cold water and the celery, onion, carrot, and bay leaves in a medium saucepan. Bring to a boil over high heat, then lower the heat and simmer for 20 minutes. Strain out the vegetables and discard; return the broth to the pan.

ADD THE CHICK-PEAS to the broth and bring to a simmer over medium-high heat. Reduce the heat to medium low, and cook until the beans are soft and creamy, 30 to 40 minutes, adding more water if needed. Add the salt.

FOR THE HERB COULIS, put the mint, cilantro, parsley, garlic, lemon juice, salt, red pepper flakes, and olive oil in a food processor or blender and purée until the mixture is smooth and light green. If the mixture is too dry to purée, add a small amount of water.

FOR THE BEURRE FONDUE, add the butter and cream to a pot and heat until the butter melts. Remove from the heat and add the lemon zest. Let stand for about 1 minute. Pour into a blender and blend until smooth. Return the mixture to the pot and add the lemon sections, salt, and pepper. Heat until the mixture begins to steam, about 135°F on a meat thermometer.

ADD THE PRAWNS to the beurre fondue and cook for about 5 minutes.

TO SERVE, drizzle each of 6 individual plates with the herb coulis and pile the chick-peas near the center of the plate. Top with the poached prawns and a drizzle of the beurre fondue.

MAKES 6 SERVINGS

localicious

Organic, sustainable, green, natural—with so many ways to describe food that is good for you and the environment, it can be hard to keep up. Now we have a new catchphrase in the mix: eating local. The world has become transfixed by the ever growing oil crisis, and the cost and environmental impact of transporting our groceries from thousands of miles away. Eating locally may be the newest buzz, but ignore the hype and do it just because it makes good, old-fashioned common sense. That tomato you get from the farm on the other side of town, your neighborhood P-patch, or the big pot sitting on your deck not only has fewer "food miles," it tastes better too. This is because it is fresh from the bush and not picked underripe only to spend weeks (or more) wrapped in plastic and sitting in a cargo hold before hitting grocery store shelves.

By visiting farmers markets that run year-round, you'll always find fresh fruits at the peak of the season; meats and cheeses from animals treated with the respect they deserve; and a wide variety of perky, vividly colored vegetables and greens that will keep your dinners from ever getting boring. Each season brings a new treat to anticipate, like tender spears of asparagus in the spring; sweet, juicy cherries in the early summer; and crisp, tart apples in the fall.

A little preplanning can help branch the leaner months early in the year when winter stores are running thin and the spring season hasn't quite dawned. Get your start in early summer by freezing large batches of strawberries when you grow tired of eating them day after day—you'll appreciate your efforts when you're craving strawberry shortcake in late fall. When tomatoes roll their way into town, pull out your biggest stockpot, and try canning your own tomato sauce, which will be a welcome treat through the dark days of winter.

If you find that your kitchen imagination (or supplies) are running low, support the movement by dining at one of many restaurants (like Vancouver's Raincity Grill, Portland's Wildwood, and Seattle's Sitka & Spruce) with menus that feature only the best of the season. After all, your asparagus really shouldn't be a more seasoned traveler than you are.

risotto alla veneziana with seared scallops and asparagus

CIOPPINO'S ❖ VANCOUVER, BRITISH COLUMBIA

Executive chef and restaurateur Giuseppe "Pino" Posteraro looks to balance his dishes with fresh flavors that aren't overpowering, such as this happy marriage of earth and sea. Use sweet, tender spring asparagus and be careful not to overcook it for best results.

1 quart prawn stock or vegetable stock

12 jumbo scallops

Salt and freshly ground black pepper

4 tablespoons extra-virgin olive oil

½ onion, finely chopped

1⅛ cups (about 9 ounces) arborio rice

2 tablespoons dry white wine, such Chenin Blanc

1 pinch saffron

Zest of 1 lemon

1 teaspoon capers

8 asparagus spears, blanched and cut on the bias into 1-inch pieces

1 tablespoon unsalted butter

1 teaspoon balsamic vinegar

WARM THE PRAWN STOCK over low heat. Meanwhile, prepare the scallops by rinsing and patting them dry with a paper towel. If the scallops are thicker than ½ inch, slice them horizontally into ½-inch rounds. Season well with salt and pepper, and set aside.

HEAT 2 TABLESPOONS of the olive oil in a medium saucepan over medium heat. Add the onion and cook until translucent, about 2 minutes. Add the rice and cook, stirring constantly, until the rice becomes translucent, 6 to 8 minutes. Add the wine and cook until the liquid evaporates. Add the stock to the rice, one ladleful at a time, stirring between each addition until the liquid has been absorbed. Stir from the center of the pot toward the sides. Add the saffron, lemon zest, and capers. When the risotto has reached a creamy texture, about 16 to 18 minutes from adding the first ladleful, add the lemon zest and asparagus. Season with salt and pepper to taste. Remove from the heat.

HEAT THE REMAINING olive oil in a nonstick frying pan over medium-high heat. Add the scallops and sear for about 2 minutes. Turn the scallops and add the butter, allowing it to sizzle until it becomes brown. Remove from the heat.

TO SERVE, place a scoop of risotto in the center of each plate, and place 3 or 4 scallops around the risotto. Stir the balsamic vinegar into the browned butter, then drizzle the mixture over the scallops.

MAKES 4 SERVINGS

seared sea scallops with huckleberry-lavender vinaigrette and chanterelle salad

COLUMBIA GORGE HOTEL ❧ HOOD RIVER, OREGON

"The stars of this recipe are three of the foods we are blessed with in the Northwest: seafood, wild mushrooms, and berries," says the hotel's former chef Britton Unketer. So it's best to prepare this recipe in late summer or early fall, when chanterelle mushrooms are in season. Or use morel mushrooms as a spring substitute. Look for weathervane sea scallops, our largest Northwest scallop. Note that the lavender oil needs to marinate for two hours.

Huckleberry-Lavender Vinaigrette

1 cup vegetable oil

½ cup fresh or edible dried lavender, stems discarded, leaves and flowers minced

½ cup huckleberries (fresh or frozen)

¼ cup white vinegar

Salt and freshly ground black pepper

Chanterelle Salad

2 tablespoons vegetable oil

5 ounces chanterelle mushrooms, cleaned and trimmed, quartered if large

4 cups baby salad greens, rinsed and dried

✄

½ cup flour

1 teaspoon freshly ground black pepper

1½ pounds sea scallops

2 tablespoons vegetable oil

FOR THE VINAIGRETTE, combine the oil and lavender in a small jar with a tight-fitting lid; shake well. Let the oil sit at room temperature for 2 hours, then strain off and discard the lavender. Return the oil to the jar. In a blender, purée the huckleberries with the vinegar until smooth. Strain the purée, then add it to the lavender oil, cover, and shake to mix well. Season to taste with salt and pepper and set aside.

FOR THE CHANTERELLE SALAD, heat the oil in a medium skillet over high heat, add the mushrooms, and sauté until just tender, 7 to 8 minutes. Transfer the mushrooms to a large bowl and add the salad greens and ⅓ cup of the vinaigrette. Toss gently to mix well. Season to taste with salt and pepper.

JUST BEFORE SERVING, combine the flour and pepper and lightly coat each scallop in the flour, patting to remove excess. Heat the oil in a large, heavy skillet or sauté pan over medium-high heat. Add the scallops and sear until nearly opaque, 4 to 5 minutes on each side. Do not disturb the scallops while they cook, or they will not form the distinctive seared crust.

ARRANGE THE SCALLOPS around the outer edge of 4 individual plates, and pile the chanterelle salad in the center. Drizzle some of the remaining vinaigrette over the scallops and serve immediately.

MAKES 4 SERVINGS

storing fresh mushrooms

Store fresh mushrooms in a well-ventilated container, such as an open paper bag, and refrigerate them. Because they're composed of 90 percent water, mushrooms will begin to dehydrate after several days if left at room temperature. Refrigerated in this way, they should last a week or two. When you're ready to use the them, wipe the mushrooms clean with a soft brush or damp cloth.

Both fresh and cooked mushrooms freeze well. To freeze fresh mushrooms, first clean them, then cut them in half or into ½-inch slices. Spread the slices on a baking sheet, cover, and freeze. Store the frozen mushrooms in airtight containers. Or you can sauté the fresh mushrooms in butter or olive oil until tender, then freeze them in airtight containers. These will keep up to six months.

singing scallops and other sweet sea delights

Several different theories explain how our Northwest singing scallops got their name. Some credit it to the fact that, when steamed, their lovely pink, violet, and orange shells gape, giving them the appearance of someone singing. Others say it's because the scallops look like mouths singing in the water when they swim—which, like most scallops, they do by opening and closing their shells. Still others maintain that singing scallops used to be called swimming scallops and someone misunderstood the name.

What seafood lovers do know is that these colorful, delicately shelled scallops—indigenous to the waters of Puget Sound, Washington Sound, the Strait of Georgia, and the Strait of Juan de Fuca—are utterly delicious. Divers harvest wild singing scallops by hand. They are also farmed commercially in northern Washington and British Columbia.

As with clams, oysters, and mussels, the entire scallop (including the orange-colored "coral" or roe) is edible. Most Americans traditionally eat only the adductor muscle—the round, fleshy disk that opens and closes the shells. The rest of the scallop spoils rapidly and is usually discarded by processors. Because of their small size and delicate flavor, singing scallops are relished whole in the shell, either steamed or raw, often with their coral attached (which is also considered a delicacy).

Other Northwest scallops include the large weathervane sea scallop, the tiny Oregon bay scallop, and the giant purple-hinged rock scallop, which, unlike other scallops, is not free-swimming. Scallops cannot hold their shells firmly closed like other bivalves, and they quickly lose body moisture when removed from the water, so scallops in the shell must be very fresh. Shucked scallops will hold for a few days if well wrapped to prevent moisture loss. Scallops cook very quickly and are best slightly undercooked rather than overcooked.

Some processors soak sea scallops in sodium tripolyphosphates (STPP) to help prevent moisture loss. STPP also retards the growth of bacteria and removes any "fishy" odor. Unfortunately, this treatment results in a bland scallop that loses water during cooking. STPP-treated scallops are very white and limp, have no odor, and stay separated in the package. Untreated scallops have a sweet sea odor, an ivory-yellow color, a firm texture, and a sticky coating that holds them together.

linguine with crawfish and fire sauce

JAKE'S FAMOUS CRAWFISH RESTAURANT ◆ PORTLAND, OREGON

Northwest crawfish (or crayfish), a freshwater relative of the lobster, were first served by Jake's namesake, Jake Freiman, at the old Oregon Hotel in 1881. Freiman guaranteed the freshest possible crawfish by keeping an inventory thriving in small ponds he had dug in the restaurant's basement. Most crawfish, however, thrive in Northwest rivers and lake bottoms, with the largest specimens harvested from the Columbia River. Aficionados insist that our Northwest crawfish are the sweetest tasting around.

Fire Sauce

2 red bell peppers
4 ounces cream cheese
2 tablespoons grated cheddar cheese
1½ tablespoons canned chipotle chiles
4 cloves garlic, coarsely chopped
2 teaspoons minced shallot
1 teaspoon minced jalapeño pepper
½ teaspoon ground pasilla chile or other ground chile
¼ teaspoon ground cumin
¼ teaspoon Cajun seasoning
Salt

✕

¼ cup unsalted butter
1 pound crawfish tail meat
2 teaspoons minced garlic
2 teaspoons minced shallot
2 cups corn kernels
½ cup diced green bell pepper
½ cup diced red bell pepper
½ cup diced red onion
Salt and freshly ground black pepper
½ cup chicken stock (see page 108)
12 ounces dried linguine
¼ cup grated Parmesan cheese

FOR THE FIRE SAUCE, roast the red peppers over a gas flame or under the broiler, turning often, until evenly charred. Put the peppers in a paper or plastic bag, close the bag, and let sit until cool enough to handle. Peel away and discard the skin, then halve the peppers, discarding the cores and seeds. Set aside.

COMBINE THE ROASTED RED PEPPERS with the cream and cheddar cheeses, chipotles, garlic, shallot, jalapeño, pasilla, cumin, and Cajun seasoning in a food processor or blender and process until smooth. Season to taste with salt and set aside.

BRING A LARGE SAUCEPAN of lightly salted water to a boil.

HEAT THE BUTTER in a large sauté pan, add the crawfish, garlic, and shallot, and sauté, stirring, for 1 to 2 minutes. Stir in the corn, peppers, and onion and season to taste with salt and pepper. Continue cooking until the vegetables are just tender, 3 to 4 minutes longer. Add the chicken stock and the fire sauce and stir until heated through.

WHEN THE WATER BOILS, add the linguine and cook until al dente, 5 to 7 minutes. Drain well and put the pasta in a large bowl. Pour the sauce over the pasta, toss well, and arrange the pasta on 4 individual plates, distributing the crawfish evenly. Sprinkle each plate with the Parmesan and serve.

MAKES 4 SERVINGS

cioppino d'oro

BUGATTI'S RISTORANTE ✦ WEST LINN, OREGON

Chef Lydia Bugatti, who relies on the freshness of ingredients and on cooking from the heart, offers her recipe for a spicy stew of Northwest seafood. A rich, creamy white wine, such as a Chateau Ste. Michelle chardonnay, makes a delightful companion for the sweet, complex seafood flavors of this cioppino. You can streamline your shopping list by choosing just three or four of the seafood varieties listed here, increasing their quantities slightly.

1 cup fish stock (see page 75) or chicken stock (see page 108)
2 pinches saffron threads
1 cup couscous
1 tablespoon olive oil
2 tablespoons chopped anchovies (about 1 can)
½ teaspoon dried red pepper flakes
1 tablespoon minced garlic
¾ cup finely shredded basil leaves
¾ cup chopped plum (Roma) tomato
1½ cups white wine
1 pound mussels, cleaned and debearded
1 pound small clams, scrubbed
¾ pound salmon fillet, skin and bones removed, cut into 1-inch cubes
½ pound halibut or rockfish fillet, skin and bones removed, cut into 1-inch cubes
½ pound medium or large shrimp, peeled and deveined
4 ounces bay scallops
4 ounces cooked bay shrimp
Basil leaves, for garnish

HEAT THE STOCK in a small saucepan until warm, crush one pinch of the saffron threads over it, remove from the heat, and let sit for 30 minutes. Bring the stock to a boil and pour it over the couscous in a large serving bowl (the seafood will be added to this bowl later). Cover the bowl and let sit for 5 minutes. Drizzle 1 teaspoon of the olive oil over the couscous and stir with a fork to separate the grains and evenly coat them in oil. Set aside.

HEAT THE REMAINING 2 teaspoons of olive oil in a large sauté pan or skillet over medium heat. Add the anchovies and sauté, stirring constantly, until they fall apart, 1 to 2 minutes. Stir in the dried red pepper flakes, garlic, basil, tomato, wine, and remaining pinch of saffron, in that order.

ADD THE MUSSELS and clams to the broth, cover the pan, and bring just to a boil. Lower the heat and simmer until the shellfish begin to open, 3 to 5 minutes. As they open, transfer the clams and mussels to the bowl with the couscous; cover the bowl to keep warm. When all the shellfish have opened (discard any that don't open after 10 minutes), add the salmon, halibut, raw shrimp, and scallops. Cover the pan and continue cooking until the seafood is just cooked through, 5 to 7 minutes, stirring in the bay shrimp at the last minute just to heat through. Taste the broth for seasoning. Carefully ladle the broth and seafood into the bowl with the couscous, garnish with basil leaves, and serve.

MAKES 4 TO 6 SERVINGS

chanterelle risotto cakes

THE BAY CAFÉ ◆ LOPEZ ISLAND, WASHINGTON

At the Bay Café, these savory wild chanterelle and rice cakes are served alongside filet mignon or grilled shrimp. But topped with sautéed mushrooms, they would also make a fine main course.

5 cups chicken stock (see page 108)

½ cup dry white wine

2 tablespoons minced flat-leaf (Italian) parsley

3 tablespoons olive oil

4 tablespoons unsalted butter, plus more if needed

1 bunch green onions, minced

2 cloves garlic, minced

½ pound golden chanterelle mushrooms, cleaned, trimmed, and thinly sliced

1½ cups arborio rice

½ cup grated Parmesan cheese, plus more for garnish

Salt and freshly ground black pepper

1 cup finely shredded spinach leaves, for garnish

¼ cup toasted pine nuts, for garnish

COMBINE THE STOCK, wine, and parsley in a medium saucepan and bring just to a low simmer.

HEAT THE OIL and 3 tablespoons of the butter in a large, heavy skillet over medium heat. Add the green onions and garlic and sauté until they begin to soften, about 3 minutes. Add the chanterelles and continue sautéing, stirring often, until the mushrooms have released their juices, 4 to 5 minutes longer. Stir in the rice until it is evenly glossy.

ADD 1 CUP of the hot stock to the rice and cook over medium heat, stirring constantly, until all of the liquid is absorbed. Continue adding stock, 1 cup at a time, about every 5 minutes, allowing the rice to absorb each addition before adding the next. When all the stock has been absorbed and the rice is tender, remove the pan from the heat and stir in the Parmesan. Season to taste with salt and pepper and let cool.

MAIN DISHES

WHEN COOL, form the risotto into cakes, using ½ cup for each, and making them about 3½ inches across and ½ inch thick. Lay the cakes on a baking sheet lined with plastic wrap, cover with a second sheet of plastic wrap, and refrigerate for 2 hours.

JUST BEFORE SERVING, heat the remaining 1 tablespoon butter in a large skillet, preferably nonstick. When the butter is melted and begins to foam, add some of the risotto cakes in a single layer; do not crowd the pan. Cook the cakes over medium-high heat until well browned and crusty, about 3 minutes on each side. Transfer the risotto cakes to a platter and keep warm while frying the remaining cakes, adding more butter as needed.

ARRANGE THE RISOTTO CAKES on plates, sprinkle with spinach, Parmesan, and pine nuts, and serve.

MAKES 4 TO 6 SERVINGS

tomato masala with paneer

VIJ'S ✿ VANCOUVER, BRITISH COLUMBIA

The best time to make this recipe is summer, when you have access to delicious, locally grown heirloom tomatoes and red onions. Paneer is a slightly labor-intensive (albeit very simple) cheese made from whole milk. You can buy ready-made paneer from most Indian grocery stores; however, it's even better made from organic milk at home. Note that you'll need a sheet of cheesecloth that, folded into 3 layers, is large enough to line a colander.

1 gallon organic whole milk

1½ teaspoons granulated sugar

⅓ cup white vinegar

½ cup olive or grapeseed oil

1 teaspoon black mustard seeds

2 pounds organic red onions, sliced

2 pounds organic tomatoes, chopped

1 teaspoon turmeric

2 teaspoons salt

1 teaspoon cayenne pepper

½ to ¾ cup chopped cilantro, stems included, plus more for garnish

TO MAKE THE PANEER, first pour ¼ cup of water into a large, heavy-bottomed pan. Then slowly pour in the entire gallon of milk. Stir in the sugar. Turn on the heat to medium and bring the milk to a boil for 15 to 20 minutes, stirring occasionally to keep from scorching. Watch constantly, and when the surface begins to foam up, but before it overflows, pour in the vinegar and remove from the heat. The foaming will subside and solids will separate from the liquid. Wait 5 minutes, until the liquid has completely separated from the solids.

LINE A COLANDER with the triple-layered cheesecloth. Place the colander in the sink and carefully pour in the entire contents of the pan. Let stand about 5 minutes to drain. Wrap the cheesecloth around the paneer in a ball shape and tie in a double knot. Place the ball of paneer, still wrapped in cheesecloth, on a large plate (on a counter or in the sink) and place a 2-quart pan filled with water on top of the paneer. This will flatten the paneer to about 2 inches thick and press out more water, making the cheese firmer. After 30 minutes, remove the pan of water. (For even firmer paneer, let it remain under the pan of water for 1 hour.) Unwrap the paneer, carefully scraping off with a spoon any that adheres to the cheesecloth, and place it on another plate.

CUT THE PANEER into 1½-inch cubes. If the paneer isn't firm enough to slice, cut a baguette or other firm-crusted bread into diagonal slices and spread with the paneer.

TO PREPARE THE TOMATO MASALA, heat the oil in a medium sauté pan over medium heat for 1 minute. Add the mustard seeds and stir until they begin to pop. Immediately add the onions and sauté until the edges begin to turn golden, 5 to 8 minutes. Stir in the tomatoes. Add the turmeric, salt, and cayenne. Stir well and sauté for 5 minutes, stopping before the tomatoes lose their shape. Remove from the heat and stir in the cilantro.

TO SERVE, ladle the hot tomato masala over the paneer. Garnish with a bit more cilantro.

MAKES 6 SERVINGS

pumpkin gnocchi in roasted vegetable pesto cream sauce

IL PIATTO ✣ PORTLAND, OREGON

Delicately colored and flavored with pumpkin, these tender potato dumplings (gnocchi) are served in a cream sauce flavored with a sweet, earthy roasted vegetable pesto. Any leftover pesto can be saved for the next day's pasta.

Roasted Vegetable Pesto

½ pound carrots, peeled, halved if large
½ pound onions, peeled and quartered
3 red bell peppers, cored, seeded, and quartered
¾ cup olive oil
½ cup grated Asiago cheese
3 tablespoons minced garlic
Salt and freshly ground black pepper

✖

2 pounds baking potatoes, scrubbed
2 teaspoons unsalted butter
1 cup chopped onion
2 tablespoons chopped garlic
3 cups flour, plus more for rolling gnocchi
½ cup pumpkin purée (fresh cooked or canned)
2 eggs
1 tablespoon salt
1 teaspoon freshly grated nutmeg
2 cups half-and-half

PREHEAT THE OVEN to 400°F.

FOR THE ROASTED VEGETABLE PESTO, arrange the carrots, onions, and red peppers in a baking dish and drizzle about ¼ cup of the olive oil over them. Roast the vegetables until lightly browned and tender, about 30 minutes.

TRANSFER THE VEGETABLES with their juices to a food processor or food mill and process until very smooth. With the machine running, slowly pour in the remaining ½ cup olive oil, then add the cheese and garlic. Season to taste with salt and pepper; set aside.

PUT THE POTATOES in a large pan with lightly salted water to cover. Bring to a boil and simmer until the potatoes are tender when pierced with a knife, 20 to 30 minutes, depending on their size.

WHILE THE POTATOES are cooking, heat the butter in a medium skillet, add the onion and garlic, and sauté over medium heat, stirring frequently, until tender, about 5 minutes.

DRAIN THE POTATOES and let sit until cool enough to handle. Peel away the skin and purée the potatoes in a ricer or with a potato masher. Stir in the sautéed onion and garlic with the flour, pumpkin, eggs, salt, and nutmeg. Stir until well mixed, then knead the mixture to form a smooth dough, 1 to 2 minutes.

LIGHTLY FLOUR YOUR HANDS and the work surface. Break off a large piece of dough and roll it into a cylinder about ½ inch in diameter. Cut into slices ½ inch thick and set the gnocchi aside on a tray lined with parchment paper or foil. Repeat with the remaining dough.

BRING THE HALF-AND-HALF to a boil in a medium skillet. Add the vegetable pesto and season to taste with salt and pepper. Set aside, covered, to keep warm.

BRING A LARGE PAN of salted water to a boil and gently drop in the gnocchi, a handful at a time. Simmer the gnocchi until they rise to the surface, 2 to 3 minutes. Scoop them out with a slotted spoon and put them in a large bowl of cold water to halt cooking. Continue cooking the remaining gnocchi.

DRAIN THE COOKED GNOCCHI WELL, add them to the warm sauce, and simmer for a few minutes to heat through. Transfer to a serving bowl or individual plates and serve immediately.

MAKES 6 TO 8 SERVINGS

quinoa-stuffed delicata squash

NEARLY NORMAL'S GONZO CUISINE ❖ CORVALLIS, OREGON

Quinoa (pronounced "keen-wa") is a tiny, millet-like seed that is cooked much like other grains. It is available in most health food stores. Delicata is a sweet, smooth-textured squash. If you can't find it, substitute another variety, such as acorn squash.

3 Delicata squash (about 1 pound each)
1½ cups quinoa
3 cups water
½ teaspoon salt
2 tablespoons vegetable oil
1 cup finely chopped celery
1 cup finely chopped onion
½ cup finely chopped red bell pepper
4 teaspoons minced garlic, plus more to taste
1 tablespoon minced fresh marjoram, or 1½ teaspoons dried
¼ teaspoon ground cardamom
Salt
1½ cups grated fontina or other semi-soft cheese

PREHEAT THE OVEN to 375°F.

HALVE THE SQUASH lengthwise and scoop out and discard the seeds. Set the squash cut side down in a roasting pan or rimmed baking sheet. Add ¼ inch of water to the pan and bake the squash until tender when pierced with a fork, 20 to 30 minutes (other types of squash may take longer). Leave the oven set at 375°F.

WHILE THE SQUASH BAKES, put the quinoa in a medium saucepan with the water and salt. Bring to a boil, reduce the heat, and simmer, covered, until all the water has been absorbed, about 15 minutes. Set aside.

HEAT THE OIL in a large saucepan. Add the celery, onion, bell pepper, garlic, marjoram, and cardamom and sauté, stirring, until tender, about 5 minutes. Remove from the heat, stir in the quinoa, and add salt to taste.

SET THE SQUASH cut side up on a dry baking sheet. Fill each half with the quinoa mixture and sprinkle the fontina on top. Bake until the filling is bubbly and lightly browned, 15 to 18 minutes. Serve immediately.

MAKES 6 SERVINGS

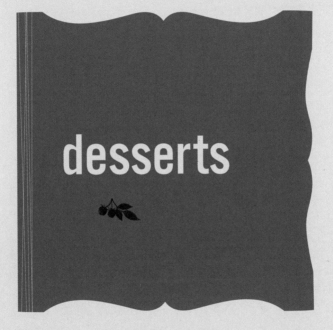

desserts

nootka rose petal ice cream

FRIDAY HARBOR HOUSE ✦ SAN JUAN ISLAND, WASHINGTON

During the summer months, San Juan Island erupts with a festival of flowers. None are more fragrant than the tiny native Nootka rose, with its compelling, spicy scent. Not all rose petals can create the delicate flavor of this ice cream; they must be richly aromatic. If you can't gather your own wild rose petals, chef Greg Atkinson recommends using unsprayed dried rosebuds from France, sold at specialty stores throughout the Northwest.

2 cups milk
2 cups fresh, unsprayed fragrant rose petals or ⅔ cup dried
6 egg yolks
1 cup sugar
2 cups whipping cream, chilled

COMBINE THE MILK and rose petals in a saucepan and bring to a boil over medium heat. As soon as the milk boils, remove the pan from the heat; let stand for 10 minutes.

STIR TOGETHER the egg yolks and sugar in a medium bowl. Strain the milk into the yolk mixture, stirring to mix. Discard the rose petals and wipe out the pan if necessary. Return the mixture to the saucepan and cook over medium-low heat until the custard is thick enough to coat the back of a spoon, 5 to 7 minutes. Do not let the custard boil or it will curdle.

LET THE CUSTARD COOL SLIGHTLY, then refrigerate until chilled. Stir in the whipping cream, pour the mixture into an ice cream maker, and freeze according to the manufacturer's instructions. Transfer the frozen ice cream to an airtight freezer container and freeze for at least 1 hour before serving.

MAKES ABOUT 1½ QUARTS

bay leaf crème brûlée

THE HERBFARM • WOODINVILLE, WASHINGTON

The Herbfarm's former chef Jerry Traunfeld loves the nutmeg-like flavor that fresh bay leaves impart to dishes. Like many herbs, he explains, bay leaves have a notably different quality when used fresh rather than dried. If you'd like to grow your own fragrant bay laurel tree, look for one at your favorite nursery. Other herbs lend themselves to this recipe as well, including lavender, rosemary, and rose geranium. Traunfeld suggests using superfine sugar for caramelizing the tops of these custards, because the fine grains melt and caramelize more evenly. You can buy it, or pulverize granulated sugar in your food processor or blender.

2 cups milk
2 cups whipping cream
12 fresh bay leaves
½ vanilla bean, split, or 1 teaspoon vanilla extract
3 whole eggs
5 egg yolks
¾ cup granulated sugar
Pinch salt
½ cup superfine sugar

BRING THE MILK and whipping cream to a boil in a medium saucepan over medium heat. Coarsely tear the fresh bay leaves and add them to the mixture along with the vanilla bean (if using). Remove the pan from the heat and let steep for 1 hour.

PREHEAT THE OVEN to 325°F.

BEAT THE EGGS, egg yolks, granulated sugar, vanilla extract (if using), and salt in a large bowl. Whisk in the steeped milk mixture until well blended. Strain the mixture through a fine sieve, discarding the bay leaves and vanilla bean.

POUR THE CUSTARD into eight ¾-cup ramekins and set them in a shallow pan filled with 1 inch of hot water. Bake the custards until just set but still slightly jiggly, 40 to 45 minutes. Let cool, then chill the custards for several hours or overnight.

JUST BEFORE SERVING, sprinkle the surface of each custard with superfine sugar, pouring off any excess. Using a small propane torch or your broiler, caramelize the sugar just until nicely browned. Serve immediately.

MAKES 8 SERVINGS

DESSERTS

zabaglione with figs, blackberries, and honey sauce

PAZZO RISTORANTE ✦ PORTLAND, OREGON

Few desserts are as ethereal yet satisfying as a traditional Italian zabaglione—a rich egg custard flavored with marsala wine. At Pazzo, zabaglione reaches several steps closer to heaven with the addition of fresh figs, blackberries, and a citrus-enhanced honey sauce. When fresh figs aren't available, use large strawberries or other seasonal fruits. Both the custard and the sauce can be prepared up to 6 hours in advance and assembled with the fruits just before serving.

Zabaglione

4 egg yolks
¼ cup sugar
¼ cup marsala wine
½ cup whipping cream

Honey Sauce

1 cup white wine
½ cup honey
¼ cup freshly squeezed orange juice
2 tablespoons freshly squeezed lemon juice
½ vanilla bean, or 1 teaspoon vanilla extract

✄

6 large or 12 small fresh figs
1 pint fresh blackberries or marionberries
6 edible flowers, such as nasturtiums or violets

CHILL 6 DESSERT PLATES.

FOR THE ZABAGLIONE, whisk together the egg yolks, sugar, and marsala in a large, heatproof bowl. Set the bowl over a pan of simmering (not boiling) water, and whisk the mixture constantly until it has about tripled in volume, 8 to 10 minutes. Remove the bowl from the pan and set it in a shallow pan of ice water. Continue whisking until the mixture is cool. Whip the cream until soft peaks form, then fold the cream into the egg mixture. Refrigerate until needed, up to 6 hours before serving.

FOR THE HONEY SAUCE, combine the wine, honey, orange juice, and lemon juice in a small saucepan with the vanilla extract, if using. If using a vanilla bean, slit the half bean lengthwise, scrape out the seeds, and add them to the pan with the split bean. Bring the mixture to a boil over medium heat, and boil until the sauce is reduced to the consistency of maple syrup, about 20 minutes (it will continue to thicken as it cools). Remove and discard the split vanilla bean and pour the sauce into a bowl. Cover and refrigerate until needed.

JUST BEFORE SERVING, cut large figs into 4 wedges, small figs in half. Spoon the chilled zabaglione onto the center of the chilled plates. Arrange the figs and berries around the zabaglione and drizzle the honey sauce over all. Garnish each plate with an edible flower and serve immediately.

MAKES 6 SERVINGS

peanut butter pie

COLOPHON CAFE ◆ BELLINGHAM, WASHINGTON

Enjoy this creamy peanut butter pie with a favorite book and you'll be true to its origin—a popular bookstore cafe. Use a metal soup spoon to help press the cookie crust into the pan—it won't stick to the crumbs as your fingers will.

8 ounces chocolate wafers, finely crushed (about 2 cups)
¼ cup unsalted butter, melted
1½ cups whipping cream
8 ounces cream cheese, softened
¾ cup chunky peanut butter
¾ cup packed brown sugar
½ teaspoon vanilla extract
¼ cup powdered sugar
4 ounces semisweet chocolate, coarsely chopped
1 tablespoon chopped peanuts

PREHEAT THE OVEN to 350°F.

COMBINE THE COOKIE CRUMBS and butter in a bowl and mix well. Pour the mixture into an 8-inch pie pan and press it evenly onto the bottom and sides. Bake until set, 7 to 10 minutes. Set aside to cool.

PUT 1 CUP of the whipping cream in a medium bowl, preferably stainless steel, and freeze for 10 minutes. Meanwhile, beat the cream cheese, peanut butter, and brown sugar together in another bowl until creamy.

TAKE THE WHIPPING CREAM from the freezer, add the vanilla, and beat with an electric mixer on low speed for 2 minutes or by hand with a whisk until smooth. Add the powdered sugar and beat until soft peaks form. Do not overbeat.

FOLD THE WHIPPED CREAM into the peanut butter mixture. Pour the filling into the crust, smoothing out the top. Freeze for at least 3 hours.

WHEN THE PIE IS FROZEN, combine the chocolate and the remaining ½ cup whipping cream in a small microwave-safe bowl and microwave for 30 to 45 seconds. Stir

until smooth; let cool. Alternatively, gently heat the chocolate and cream together in a small pan over medium-low heat until the chocolate is nearly melted; remove from the heat, stir until smooth, and let cool slightly.

TAKE THE FROZEN PIE from the freezer and spread the chocolate topping over it. Sprinkle the chopped peanuts on top before the chocolate sets. If not serving right away, return the pie to the freezer. One hour before serving, take the pie out of the freezer and put it in the refrigerator. Use a knife dipped in hot water to cut the pie; it is easier to cut if still partially frozen.

MAKES 8 SERVINGS

espresso cheesecake

TURTLEBACK FARM INN ✦ ORCAS ISLAND, WASHINGTON

A slice of indulgence is often good for the soul. Packed with everything we usually try to avoid—cream cheese, Kahlua, espresso, butter, and more—this luscious dessert is one that's tough to turn down. Note that this cheesecake should be made a day before serving.

>8 ounces chocolate wafers, finely crushed (about 2 cups)
>¼ cup unsalted butter, melted
>2 pounds cream cheese, softened
>3 eggs
>¾ cup packed brown sugar
>½ cup sour cream
>¼ cup Kahlua or other coffee liqueur
>¼ cup strong espresso, cooled
>1 teaspoon vanilla extract
>¾ teaspoon salt

PREHEAT THE OVEN to 350°F. Lightly grease an 8- or 9-inch springform pan.

STIR TOGETHER the crushed cookies and melted butter. Press the crumb mixture evenly onto the bottom and sides of the springform pan. Set aside.

BEAT THE CREAM CHEESE in the large bowl of an electric mixer until smooth and creamy. Add the eggs, followed by the brown sugar, sour cream, Kahlua, espresso, vanilla, and salt. When thoroughly blended and smooth, pour the filling into the prepared crust and bake until set (the center should not shudder when the pan is gently shaken), 60 to 70 minutes. Let cool thoroughly, then chill overnight before serving. To serve, remove the rim of the springform pan and cut the cheesecake into wedges.

MAKES 10 TO 12 SERVINGS

coffee culture

How coffee became a Northwest claim to fame may never be completely understood, especially since no coffee tree worth its beans could produce the potent fruit in such a cool and temperate climate. Still, coffee roasters large and small have put down their roots here and have redefined a good cuppa joe. When people think of the Northwest, they think of coffee. Coffee production these days is akin to microbrewing and producing boutique wine, with true artisans at the helm who are passionate about everything from bean selection to getting the perfect microfoam to creating latte art masterpieces.

The most important part of a quality cup, whether you plan to drink it or cook with it, is starting with great-tasting beans and using them while they are fresh. Ignore the rumors about preserving coffee beans in the freezer, and instead buy your beans in small batches freshly roasted. Always use them within three to ten days after roasting. Look for coffee roasters that stamp the roasting date right on the package (Stumptown Coffee and many others do this) or head into one of the many microroasters in the area for a free coffee cupping to learn more about the characteristics of beans grown in varying climates and altitudes, or about the complexities of blending beans. The only real danger is that you may never be able to tolerate that gas station coffee again.

chocolate soufflé tarts

BUGATTI'S RISTORANTE ◆ WEST LINN, OREGON

Topped with a fluffy cloud of barely sweet whipped cream and warm bittersweet chocolate sauce, these intensely flavored individual chocolate soufflé tarts are a sophisticated dessert indulgence.

1¼ cups sugar

½ cup milk

7 ounces high-quality unsweetened chocolate, such as Callebaut or Valrhona, coarsely chopped

3 whole eggs, separated

2 egg whites

Pinch cream of tartar

Whipped Cream
1 cup whipping cream

1 teaspoon sugar

Warm Chocolate Sauce
4 ounces high-quality semisweet chocolate, such as Callebaut or Valrhona, coarsely chopped

½ cup whipping cream

PREHEAT THE OVEN to 400°F.

HEAT 1 CUP of the sugar with the milk in a medium saucepan until the sugar has dissolved, stirring occasionally. Bring just to a boil, add the unsweetened chocolate, remove from the heat, and stir until the chocolate is melted. Let cool for 10 minutes.

LIGHTLY GREASE eight 4-inch tartlet tins and set them on a baking sheet.

BEAT THE 5 EGG WHITES with the cream of tartar until soft peaks form. Add the remaining ¼ cup sugar, and continue beating until stiff and glossy.

STIR THE EGG YOLKS into the chocolate mixture, then gently fold the chocolate mixture into the egg whites, a third at a time. Pour the batter into the prepared tartlet tins, filling them to about ¼ inch from the top. Bake until the tops are puffed and starting to split, 12 to 15 minutes; do not open the oven door during baking.

WHILE THE TARTS are baking, whip the cream with the sugar until soft peaks form. Chill until needed.

FOR THE CHOCOLATE SAUCE, combine the semisweet chocolate and whipping cream in a small saucepan and warm over low heat, stirring often, until the chocolate has melted and the sauce is smooth. Keep warm.

LET THE TARTS sit for a few minutes before unmolding. Set them on individual plates, drizzle the warm chocolate sauce over them, and top each with a dollop of whipped cream. Serve immediately.

MAKES 8 SERVINGS

yam pie with pecan pralines

SEL GRIS ◆ PORTLAND, OREGON

We may live in the Northwest, but there is nothing wrong with indulging in a little deep South tradition with Sel Gris's take on sweet-potato pie. Red Garnet yams (which are actually sweet potatoes, not true yams) have a smooth reddish skin and develop a rich bronze color when baked. You can substitute any sweet potato in this recipe, but the red Garnets make for the most flavorful and creamy filling.

One packaged 10-inch deep-dish pie crust

Yam Filling
2 large red Garnet yams
¾ cup brown sugar
3 eggs
3 tablespoons melted unsalted butter, cooled to room temperature
One 12-ounce can evaporated milk
1 teaspoon vanilla extract
½ teaspoon salt
¾ teaspoon cinnamon
½ teaspoon freshly grated nutmeg
½ teaspoon freshly grated ginger
½ teaspoon allspice

Pecan Pralines
1½ cups pecan halves
1 cup light brown sugar
½ cup granulated sugar
½ teaspoon vanilla extract
½ cup whipping cream
4 tablespoons (½ stick) unsalted butter

Whipped Cream
2 cups whipping cream
1 teaspoon vanilla
3 tablespoons granulated sugar

HALF-BAKE THE PIE CRUST according to the package instructions. Set aside.

HEAT THE OVEN to 350°F.

COVER THE YAMS IN FOIL and bake until completely soft, 1 to 1½ hours. Allow the yams to cool, then peel, but keep the oven heated to 350°F.

TO MAKE THE PECAN PRALINES, spread the pecan halves in a baking pan and toast until they are crisp and aromatic, about 10 minutes. Keep the oven heated to 350°F.

LIGHTLY COAT a sheet of baking parchment or foil or another baking sheet with cooking spray. Combine the sugars, vanilla, cream, butter, and 2 tablespoons of water in a heavy sauté pan. Bring to a boil over medium-high heat, stirring constantly until the mixture reaches 240°F. Moving quickly, add the warm pecans and remove from the heat. Stir until the pecans stay suspended in the candy, about 2 minutes. Pour onto the sprayed paper, foil, or cookie sheet and let cool. Break into smaller pieces if necessary.

IN A FOOD PROCESSOR or blender, blend the yams, brown sugar, eggs, melted butter, evaporated milk, vanilla, salt, cinnamon, nutmeg, ginger, and allspice until smooth. Pour into the half-baked pie shell. Bake until set, 75 to 95 minutes.

SET THE PIE on a wire rack and let cool to room temperature, then refrigerate.

TO SERVE, whip together the cream, vanilla, and sugar until soft peaks form. Spread or pipe the whipped cream over the pie and scatter with the pecan pralines.

MAKES 8 TO 10 SERVINGS

sweet potato hazelnut poundcake

WILDWOOD • PORTLAND, OREGON

Dense, sweet, and moist, this pound cake is delicious served with vanilla ice cream or caramel sauce. Note that the sweet potato needs to be baked a day ahead. If you like, dust the cake with powdered sugar just before serving.

1 large sweet potato (about 1 pound)

1¾ cups flour

½ teaspoon baking powder

½ teaspoon salt

½ teaspoon freshly grated nutmeg

½ teaspoon ground cinnamon

1½ cups sugar

¾ cup unsalted butter, softened

3 eggs

1 teaspoon vanilla extract

½ cup buttermilk

2 tablespoons water

½ cup hazelnuts, toasted and chopped

THE DAY BEFORE MAKING THE CAKE, preheat the oven to 350°F. Bake the sweet potato until tender, 50 to 60 minutes. When the potato is cool enough to handle, remove the skin and put the flesh in a small strainer set over a bowl. Let sit overnight in the refrigerator to allow excess liquid to drain. Mash the flesh until smooth.

PREHEAT THE OVEN to 350°F.

BUTTER A 12-INCH BUNDT PAN. Sift together the flour, baking powder, salt, nutmeg, and cinnamon. In the bowl of an electric mixer or using a large whisk, cream the sugar and butter for about 3 minutes, then add the eggs, one at a time, blending well after each addition. Stir in the vanilla extract.

COMBINE THE BUTTERMILK and water in a small bowl. Add this to the butter-sugar mixture, little by little, alternating with the dry ingredients, folding gently to incorporate each addition. Fold in the hazelnuts and mashed sweet potato last. Pour the batter into the prepared pan, spreading it out evenly. Bake until a toothpick inserted in the center comes out clean, 50 to 60 minutes. Let the cake cool, then invert it onto a platter for serving.

MAKES 10 TO 12 SERVINGS

cranberry-apple bette

WHARFSIDE BED & BREAKFAST ◆ FRIDAY HARBOR, WASHINGTON

Serve this tangy cranberry "bette" warm from the oven for dessert (or even breakfast). Tart, firm apples, such as Granny Smiths, Fujis, or Gravensteins, are recommended.

6 tablespoons unsalted butter

4 cups finely cubed soft bread, preferably sourdough

5 cups peeled, sliced baking apples (4 to 5 large apples)

1 cup packed brown sugar

¾ teaspoon ground nutmeg

½ teaspoon ground cinnamon

2 cups fresh or frozen cranberries (thawed if frozen)

Lemon Sauce

½ cup granulated sugar

1 tablespoon cornstarch

Pinch salt

1 cup water

1 teaspoon grated lemon zest

2 tablespoons freshly squeezed lemon juice

2 tablespoons unsalted butter

HEAT 3 TABLESPOONS of the butter in a large skillet over medium-high heat, add the bread cubes, and cook, stirring often, until the bread is browned, about 4 to 5 minutes. Set aside.

PREHEAT THE OVEN to 350°F.

ARRANGE HALF OF THE APPLE SLICES in a greased 8-inch square baking dish. In a small bowl, stir together the brown sugar, nutmeg, and cinnamon. Sprinkle half of the sugar mixture over the apples and top with half of the bread cubes. Dot the bread with 1½ tablespoons of the remaining butter, and spread the cranberries on top. Layer with the remaining apple slices, followed by the remaining sugar mixture, then the remaining bread cubes. Dot the top with the remaining 1½ tablespoons butter, cover the dish with foil, and bake for 45 minutes. Remove the foil and use the back of a spoon to press gently on the topping so that it soaks up some of the juices below. Continue baking until the top is golden brown, 15 to 20 minutes longer.

PREPARE THE LEMON SAUCE while the bette is baking. Stir together the sugar, cornstarch, and salt in a small saucepan. Add the water and lemon zest and bring to a boil. Simmer the sauce until slightly thickened, about 2 minutes. Remove from the heat, add the lemon juice and butter, and stir until the butter is melted.

WHEN THE BETTE IS DONE, remove it from the oven and let it sit for 5 minutes. Spoon the bette onto individual plates or bowls and serve warm with the lemon sauce drizzled over it.

MAKES 6 TO 8 SERVINGS

cranberries: from the bog to the table

Each autumn the Long Beach Peninsula in Southwest Washington is ablaze in scarlet and crimson as acres of cranberries hang red, ripe, and ready for harvest. Cranberries have been raised commercially on the peninsula for over a hundred years, and growers there now raise more than five million pounds of cranberries annually. Long before the commercial harvest, Native Americans gathered wild cranberries, which grew in local peat bogs and muskegs. They steam-cooked the berries or stored them in damp moss, and then pounded and mixed them with deer or elk meat and fat to make pemmican, a high-calorie food for traveling. Later, cranberries became an important trade item with early Northwest settlers.

Originally called craneberries, because the flower resembles the bill of a crane, cranberries are a low-growing member of the heath family, which also includes blueberries and salal. Most cranberries from the Long Beach Peninsula are raised and sold to cranberry giant Ocean Spray of Massachusetts.

Because of their high pectin content, cranberries jell nicely. They are packed with vitamin C, a fact known to old-time New England sea captains, who stocked them aboard ship to prevent scurvy. One-half cup of unsweetened whole cranberries contains only about 20 calories. The color in cranberries has to do with their variety, not their quality.

After purchasing cranberries, sort them without washing and place in a bowl or glass jar. Cover loosely and refrigerate. Wash just before using.

hood river pears poached in riesling and wrapped in phyllo

COLUMBIA GORGE HOTEL ◆ HOOD RIVER, OREGON

Chefs at the Columbia Gorge Hotel use an ultra-sweet Northwest late harvest riesling for poaching. They also suggest Portland-based Clear Creek Distillery's pear brandy for use in the poaching liquid and the sauce. Virtually any pears work well in this recipe, including Bartlett, Bosc, Comice, d'Anjou, and Seckel. Tip: Once sheets of phyllo dough are removed from the package, keep them covered with plastic wrap or a damp cloth to keep them moist and pliable.

6 cups (2 bottles) riesling

1 cup sugar

Zest of 1 lemon, cut into 1-inch strips

3 tablespoons pear brandy

1 small cinnamon stick

4 whole cloves

1 vanilla bean, split, or 2 teaspoons vanilla extract

¼ teaspoon freshly grated nutmeg

4 small pears, peeled and cored whole

4 sheets phyllo dough

¼ cup unsalted butter, melted

Sauce

¾ cup whipping cream

2 egg yolks

3 tablespoons pear brandy

¼ cup sugar

COMBINE THE WINE, sugar, lemon zest, pear brandy, cinnamon stick, cloves, vanilla bean or extract, and nutmeg in a deep saucepan. Bring just to a boil, stirring occasionally, then reduce to a simmer. Add the pears and cook gently over medium heat until they are just tender when pierced with a knife, 40 to 45 minutes. Remove the pears from the saucepan and drain. Strain the poaching liquid, return it to the saucepan, and boil until reduced to about ¼ cup, about 30 minutes. Remove from the heat and let cool.

FOR THE SAUCE, whip the cream until soft peaks form; set aside. In the top of a double boiler or in a stainless steel mixing bowl, combine the egg yolks, brandy, reduced poaching liquid, and sugar. Whisk the mixture over a pan of lightly simmering water until it is thick and slightly warm, 3 to 5 minutes. Do not let the mixture become too hot or the eggs will curdle. When thick, remove the mixture from the heat and continue whisking until very light, 3 to 5 minutes longer. Whisk in about one-third of the whipped cream, then gently fold in the remaining whipped cream. Chill the sauce until needed.

PREHEAT THE OVEN to 400°F.

LAY 1 SHEET of phyllo dough on the work surface and gently brush some of the melted butter on it. Lay another sheet of phyllo on top and brush more butter on it. Repeat with the remaining phyllo sheets and butter. Cut the layered sheets into 4 equal portions and set a pear upright in the center of each portion. Lift the edges of the phyllo and gently press them against the pears; brush the outside of the phyllo with butter. Set the pears on a baking sheet and bake until the phyllo is nicely browned, about 8 minutes.

SET 1 PEAR in the center of each of 4 individual plates and spoon the sauce around the pears. Serve immediately.

MAKES 4 SERVINGS

northwest pears

Unlike many fruits that ripen on the tree, pears must be picked unripe and allowed to ripen gradually at room temperature. The best way to ripen a pear is in a paper bag along with bananas or apples, which release ethylene gas that speeds the ripening process.

A pear's peak window of ripening passes very quickly—some chefs estimate it to be a mere two hours—so it's crucial to check pears often for ripeness by smelling them (ripe pears give off a delicious perfume) and by pressing down gently on the stem end. When ripe, a pear will give slightly.

Ninety-five percent of all pears grown in the United States come from Oregon, Washington, and Northern California. Others are grown in British Columbia's Okanagan Valley. Each variety has its own unique flavor and texture.

BARTLETT: This is the pear most commonly grown in the Northwest. Fresh Bartletts, with their sweet, delicate flavor, are at their peak in summer, when their deep yellow skin is often flecked with pink or green.

RED BARTLETT: A Yakima farmer was walking down a row of green Bartlett pears when he noticed a branch bearing red pears. Graftings taken from this tree (and a similar tree in Australia) are the ancestors of all red Bartletts. The flavor of these late-summer fruits is very similar to that of yellow Bartletts—delicate and sweet.

BOSC: Slow to ripen, this pear is often mistakenly thought of as tough and dry. But when ripe it is creamy, juicy, aromatic, and spicy. The Bosc is a favorite for eating fresh or for poaching, which shows off its elegant, graceful shape.

COMICE: Many consider plump, fat-bottomed Comice pears to be the most delicious of all. They are raised to perfection in Oregon's Rogue River Valley.

WINTER NELIS: According to one pear aficionado, this pear is "rough outside, but with a heart of gold." Its creamy, sweet, aromatic flesh is great for fresh eating and for baking in pies and tarts.

SECKEL: Because of their small size and homely appearance, Seckels are not often sold commercially, but they are some of the tastiest pears around. Their dense flesh is particularly sweet, making them ideal as dessert pears or snacks.

gratin of raspberries and cider sabayon with hot and cold jellies

RAINCITY GRILL ✳ VANCOUVER, BRITISH COLUMBIA

The hot and cold jellies in this dessert may push your kitchen prowess, but they make for a novel combination of sensory delights. Warm, cold, creamy, and fruity all come together in each playful spoonful. For a simpler version of this dessert, the gratin of raspberry and sabayon is an elegant dessert all on its own. The light, dry, and effervescent Merridale Estate cider makes for a refreshing accompaniment.

2 pounds fresh raspberries

3 tablespoons fireweed honey or other wildflower honey

1 quart Merridale traditional cider or other locally made, dry hard cider

4 sheets gelatin

¾ teaspoon powdered agar

Sabayon

5 egg yolks

½ cup fireweed honey or other wildflower honey

⅔ cup Merridale traditional cider or other locally made, dry hard cider

✳

½ cup mint leaves, finely sliced

½ cup basil leaves, finely sliced

WASH THE BERRIES, drain, and dry on a kitchen towel at room temperature. Make a light syrup with the 3 tablespoons honey by combining with ¼ cup water in a small saucepan and warming over low heat. When warm, remove from heat, cover, and chill.

TO MAKE THE COLD JELLY, place 1 cup of the cider in a small saucepan over low heat. In a separate small bowl, soften the gelatin sheets in 2 cups of ice water. Let sit for 5 minutes, then squeeze out the excess water. Add the gelatin sheets to the warm cider. Once the gelatin is dissolved, remove from the heat. Stir in 1 additional cup of the cider. Mix and refrigerate for at least 3 hours or overnight.

TO MAKE THE HOT JELLY, put the remaining 2 cups of cider in a small saucepan. Whisk in the agar and bring the mixture to a boil over medium heat, whisking constantly. Press through a fine sieve and chill.

TO MAKE THE SABAYON, bring a large pan of water to a simmer over medium heat. In a large metal bowl that fits into the pan of water, combine the egg yolks, honey, and cider. Set the bowl over the simmering water so the bottom of the bowl is immersed, and beat with a large whisk. Beat the mixture constantly until it reaches 185°F (85°C). Transfer the hot mixture to an electric mixer and keep beating until cool.

PREHEAT THE BROILER. Coat the raspberries with a small amount of the honey syrup. Add the mint and basil and divide among 4 small oven-safe serving bowls. Cover with the sabayon and brown the tops under the broiler to create a gratin.

CUT A THIN PIECE OF CARDBOARD into a template that will fit vertically inside a stemless red wine glass (or other individual serving glass) to divide it in half. Wrap the cardboard template in plastic wrap to make it water resistant.

REMOVE BOTH JELLIES from the refrigerator. Warm the agar jelly in a microwave, stirring every 20 seconds; the gel will remain in a set state until 176°F (80°C).

TO SERVE, place the cardboard template in one of the serving glasses. Pour the cold jelly into one side and the hot jelly into the other. Then carefully remove the divider. Repeat with the remaining 3 serving glasses. Serve alongside the raspberry gratin.

MAKES 4 SERVINGS

wild blackberry sorbet

EAGLES NEST INN ✱ LANGLEY, WASHINGTON

Native wild trailing blackberries are the favorite berry at the Eagles Nest Inn bed-and-breakfast. Unsweetened frozen blackberries can be used in place of fresh berries, but avoid berries frozen in syrup.

2 pints (4 cups) wild blackberries

1½ cups water

½ cup freshly squeezed orange juice

½ cup sugar

2 egg whites

Whole blackberries and thoroughly washed blackberry leaves, for garnish (optional)

RINSE THE BERRIES and put them in a medium saucepan with the water, orange juice, and sugar. Bring to a boil and simmer for 5 minutes. Strain off and reserve the liquid. Press the fruit through a fine sieve, using a rubber spatula or the back of a large spoon. Add this fruit purée to the reserved liquid and let cool to room temperature.

WHEN THE BLACKBERRY MIXTURE IS COOL, beat the egg whites until just stiff but not dry. While gently beating, slowly pour in the blackberry mixture until fully incorporated. Pour this sorbet base into an ice cream maker and freeze according to the manufacturer's instructions. When set, transfer the mixture to a freezer container and continue freezing until solid. Before serving, let the sorbet sit at room temperature for a few minutes to make scooping easier.

MAKES 2 QUARTS

untangling the vines: northwest berries

BLACKBERRIES

HIMALAYA BLACKBERRY (*Rubus procerus*): The Himalaya blackberry, originally a cultivated variety, has become naturalized in the Northwest and is the most prolific of our "wild" blackberries. This is a large, juicy, flavorful berry, but when cooked it is rather bland unless you add lemon juice.

PACIFIC TRAILING WILD BLACKBERRY OR DEWBERRY (*R. ursinus*): Often found growing in areas where the ground has been disturbed, this tiny, superb native berry is more flavorful and has fewer seeds than the Himalaya or evergreen blackberries.

EVERGREEN BLACKBERRY (*R. laciniatus*): Also an escapee from cultivation, this plant has deeply toothed leaves. Its berries are more round and compact than those of the Himalaya variety and have a less complex flavor.

CULTIVATED BLACKBERRIES: Blackberry hybrids include the marionberry, loganberry, tayberry, boysenberry, and Kakota berry (a recent cross developed at Oregon State University). These hybrids tend to be larger and less seedy than their wild cousins.

RASPBERRIES

WILD RASPBERRY (*R. idaeus*): These flavorful berries are a bit smaller than cultivated raspberries and grow in shades of red or yellow.

BLACK RASPBERRY OR BLACKCAP (*R. leucodemis*): This native shrub has a distinctive blue-gray bloom on the fruit and stalks. The blackish-purple berries are soft and have a distinctive, Muscat-like flavor.

THIMBLEBERRY (*R. parviflorus*): A shallow-cupped, soft, scarlet berry with a very sweet flavor, the thimbleberry should be used as soon as possible after picking.

SALMONBERRY (*R. spectabilis*): These large, fleshy berries vary from salmon and gold to deep crimson and maroon. Depending on where they grow, the flavor ranges from insipid to very sweet.

CULTIVATED RASPBERRIES: Varieties popular in the Northwest include Willamette and Meeker (a juicy early-ripening variety).

STRAWBERRIES

Several varieties of wild strawberries are native to the Northwest. All are low-growing shrubs with tiny, edible berries. The most flavorful is the coastal strawberry, Fragaria chiloensis.

The larger hybrid strawberries were first developed in the 1800s, when the large South American variety was crossed with the smaller European variety. Unlike the stalwart strawberries imported from California and New Zealand, which are bred for hardiness and are often insipid, Northwest strawberry varieties—which include Hood, Totem, Rainier, and Shuksan—are juicy and deep red throughout.

BLUEBERRIES AND THEIR RELATIVES

Most wild members of the blueberry family can be substituted for cultivated blueberries in your favorite recipe.

SALAL BERRY (Gaultheria shallon): These dark-blue to violet berries have a sweet almond-like flavor with a refreshing minty aftertaste (salal is closely related to the wintergreen plant). Northwest Natives ate salal with a special spoon made of black mountain goat horn that did not show the berry stains.

OVAL-LEAVED BLUEBERRY (Vaccinium ovalifolium): Found in deep woods at middle elevations, these round, blue berries are covered with a soft, gray bloom. They are sweet and flavorful.

EVERGREEN HUCKLEBERRY (V. ovatum): Found along the coast and in the foothills, these shiny, purple-to-blue-black berries are packed with flavor.

WILD MOUNTAIN HUCKLEBERRY OR BLACK HUCKLEBERRY (V. membranaceum): These shiny, pear-shaped blue-black berries grow in the foothills at elevations above three thousand feet. They are highly prized for baking and even winemaking.

RED HUCKLEBERRY (V. parvifolium): Translucent rose to candy-apple red, these tart berries are delicious in pies, muffins, and pancakes.

WESTERN BLUEBERRY (V. uliginosum): This blue-black berry with a slate-gray bloom grows in bogs and in the coastal mountains.

CULTIVATED BLUEBERRIES: More than fifty varieties of blueberries are cultivated in the Northwest. The first varieties available are Earliblue and Bluetta. Spartan, Bluecrop, Berkeley, and Elliot are available mid- to late season.

rhubarb crumble with buttermilk ice cream

CHRISTINA'S ⟩ ORCAS ISLAND, WASHINGTON

The tang of buttermilk counterpoints the sweetness of this rhubarb crumble. If you like the tart flavor of rhubarb, use the lesser amount of sugar suggested; if you prefer it sweeter, use more.

Buttermilk Ice Cream

2 cups whipping cream

6 egg yolks

2 cups buttermilk

2 cups sugar

1 vanilla bean or 2 teaspoons vanilla extract

✖

2 pounds rhubarb, trimmed and cut into 1-inch pieces (about 8 cups)

2½ to 3 cups granulated sugar

½ cup ginger ale

½ cup cornstarch

1 tablespoon grated or minced ginger

1 cup packed brown sugar

1 cup rolled oats

½ cup unsalted butter, softened

½ cup flour

1 teaspoon ground cinnamon

1 teaspoon ground cardamom

½ teaspoon ground cloves

FOR THE ICE CREAM, combine 1 cup of the whipping cream and the egg yolks in the top of a double boiler and set it over a pan of lightly simmering (not boiling) water. Gently heat the mixture, stirring constantly, until thickened and creamy. Remove from the heat. In another bowl, combine the remaining 1 cup whipping cream with the buttermilk and sugar. Split the vanilla bean and scrape its seeds into the bowl, discarding the rest of the vanilla bean, or add the vanilla extract. Stir in the hot mixture.

Pour the mixture into an ice cream maker and freeze according to the manufacturer's instructions. Transfer to an airtight container and freeze until set.

PREHEAT THE OVEN to 350°F. Lightly grease a 9- by 13-inch baking dish.

TOSS TOGETHER THE RHUBARB, sugar, ginger ale, cornstarch, and ginger in a large bowl until the ingredients are well mixed and the cornstarch has dissolved. Spread evenly in the baking dish.

COMBINE THE BROWN SUGAR, oats, butter, flour, cinnamon, cardamom, and cloves in another bowl. Stir until thoroughly combined. Scatter the topping evenly over the rhubarb. Bake the crumble until the top is golden and the filling is bubbling around the edges, 60 to 70 minutes. Let cool slightly before cutting into serving pieces. Serve with a generous scoop of buttermilk ice cream.

MAKES 8 SERVINGS

appendix: restaurants & inns

ABIGAIL'S HOTEL
906 McClure Street
Victoria, BC V8V 3E7
Canada
(604) 338-5363
www.abigailshotel.com

**AMY'S MANOR BED &
BREAKFAST**
435 US Highway 153
Pateros, WA 98846
(509) 923-2334

THE BAY CAFÉ
9 Old Post Road, Suite C
Lopez Island, WA 98261
(360) 468-3700
www.bay-cafe.com

THE BAY HOUSE
PO Box 847
5911 SW Highway 101
Lincoln City, OR 97367
(541) 996-3222
www.thebayhouse.org

THE BEACONSFIELD INN
998 Humboldt Street
Victoria, BC V8V 2Z8
Canada
(604) 384-4044
www.beaconsfieldinn.com

BUGATTI'S RISTORANTE
18740 Willamette Drive
West Linn, OR 97068
(503) 636-9555
www.bugattisrestaurant.com

CAFE LANGLEY
PO Box 851
113 First Street
Langley, WA 98260
(360) 221-3090
www.cafelangley.com

**CHARLES AT SMUGGLERS
COVE**
8340 53rd Avenue W
Mukilteo, WA 98275
(425) 347-2700
www.charlesatsmugglerscove.com

CHRISTINA'S
PO Box 1059
310 Main Street
Eastsound, WA 98245
(360) 376-4904
www.christinas.net

CINCIN
1154 Robson Street
Vancouver, BC V6E 1B5
Canada
(604) 688-7338
www.cincin.net

**CIOPPINO'S MEDITERRANEAN
GRILL & ENOTECA**
1133 Hamilton Street
Vancouver, BC V6B 5P6
Canada
(604) 688-7411
www.cioppinos.wordpress.com

COLOPHON CAFE
1208 11th Street
Bellingham, WA 98225
(360) 647-0092
www.colophoncafe.com

COLUMBIA GORGE HOTEL
4000 Westcliff Drive
Hood River, OR 97031
(800) 345-1921
(541) 386-5566
www.columbiagorgehotel.com

DELILAH'S
1789 Comox Street
Vancouver, BC V6G 1H7
Canada
(604) 687-3424
www.delilahs.ca

DURLACHER HOF
PO Box 1125
7055 Nesters Road
Whistler, BC V0N 1B0
Canada
(604) 932-1924
www.durlacherhof.com

EAGLES NEST INN
4680 Saratoga Road
Langley, WA 98260
(360) 221-5331
www.eaglesnestinn.com

ETTA'S SEAFOOD
2020 Western Avenue
Seattle, WA 98121
(206) 443-6000
www.tomdouglas.com/ettas

**FAIRBURN FARM COUNTRY
MANOR**
RR 7, 3310 Jackson Road
Duncan, BC V9L 4W4
Canada
(604) 746-4637

FAIRMONT CHATEAU WHISTLER
4599 Chateau Boulevard
Whistler, BC V0N 1B0
Canada
(866) 540-4424
(604) 938-8000
www.fairmont.com/whistler

THE FLYING L RANCH
25 Flying L Lane
Glenwood, WA 98619
(509) 364-3488
www.mt-adams.com

FRIDAY HARBOR HOUSE
PO Box 1385
130 West Street
Friday Harbor, WA 98250
(360) 378-8455
www.fridayharborhouse.com

GIRAFFE RESTAURANT
15053 Marine Drive
White Rock, BC V4B 1C5
Canada
(604) 538-6878
www.thegiraffe.com

GRATEFUL BREAD BAKERY & RESTAURANT
34805 Brooten Road
Pacific City, OR 97135
(503) 965-7337

GREEN GABLES INN
922 Bonsella Street
Walla Walla, WA 99362
(509) 525-5501
www.greengablesinn.com

GROVELAND COTTAGE
4861 Sequim Dungeness Way
Sequim, WA 98382
(360) 683-3565
www.grovelandcottage.com

THE HARVEST VINE
2701 E Madison Street
Seattle, WA 98112
(206) 320-9771
www.harvestvine.com

THE HEATHMAN HOTEL
1001 SW Broadway Avenue
Portland, OR 97205
(800) 551-0011
(503) 241-4100
http://portland.heathmanhotel.com

THE HERBFARM
14590 NE 145th Street
Woodinville, WA 98072
(425) 485-5300
www.herbfarm.com

IL BISTRO
93-A Pike Street
Seattle, WA 98101
(206) 682-3049
www.ilbistro.net

IL PIATTO
2348 SE Ankeny Street
Portland, OR 97214
(503) 236-4997
www.ilpiattopdx.com

THE INN AT LANGLEY
PO Box 835
400 First Street
Langley, WA 98260
(360) 221-3033
www.innatlangley.com

INN AT SWIFTS BAY
856 Port Stanley Road
Lopez Island, WA 98261
(360) 468-3636
www.swiftsbay.com

JAKE'S FAMOUS CRAWFISH RESTAURANT
401 SW 12th Avenue
Portland, OR 97205
(503) 226-1419

LA BERENGERIE
Montague Harbour Road
Galiano Island, BC V0N 1P0
Canada
(250) 539-5392
http://galiano.gulfislands.com/laberengerie

LA SERRE RESTAURANT
PO Box 286
160 W 2nd Street
Yachats, OR 97498
(541) 547-3420

LE PIGEON
738 E Burnside Street
Portland, OR 97214
(503) 546-8796
www.lepigeon.com

MAPLE LEAF GRILL
8909 Roosevelt Way NE
Seattle, WA 98115
(206) 523-8449
www.mapleleafgrill.com

MARCO'S SUPPERCLUB
2510 1st Avenue
Seattle, WA 98121
(206) 441-7801
www.marcossupperclub.com

MONSOON
615 19th Avenue E
Seattle, WA 98112
(206) 325-2111
www.monsoonseattle.com

MOUNT ASHLAND INN
550 Mt Ashland Ski Road
Ashland, OR 97520
(541) 482-8707
www.mtashlandinn.com

NEARLY NORMAL'S GONZO CUISINE
109 NW 15th Street
Corvallis, OR 97330
(541) 753-0791
www.nearlynormals.com

OCEANWOOD COUNTRY INN
630 Dinner Bay Road
Mayne Island, BC V0N 2J0
Canada
(250) 539-5074
www.oceanwood.com

THE OLD FARMHOUSE
RR 4, 1077 North End Road
Salt Spring Island, BC V0S 1E0
Canada
(250) 537-4113

OLYMPIC LIGHTS
146 Starlight Way
Friday Harbor, WA 98250
(360) 378-3186
www.olympiclights.com

PAZZO RISTORANTE
627 SW Washington Street
Portland, OR 97205
(503) 228-1515
www.pazzo.com

QUIMPER INN
1306 Franklin Street
Port Townsend, WA 98368
(360) 385-1060
www.quimperinn.com

RAINCITY GRILL
1193 Denman Street
Vancouver, BC V6G 2N1
Canada
(604) 685-7337
www.raincitygrill.com

RAM'S HEAD INN
4465 Red Mountain Road
Rossland, BC V0G 1Y0
Canada
(250) 362-9577
www.ramshead.bc.ca

RAY'S BOATHOUSE
6049 Seaview Avenue NW
Seattle, WA 98107
(206) 789-3770
www.rays.com

THE RIO CAFE
125 9th Street
Astoria, OR 97103
(503) 325-2409

RIVERPLACE HOTEL
1510 SW Harbor Way
Portland, OR 97201
(800) 227-1333
(503) 228-3233
www.riverplacehotel.com

ROMEO INN
295 Idaho Street
Ashland, OR 97520
(541) 488-0884
www.romeoinn.com

ROVER'S
2808 E Madison Street
Seattle, WA 98112
(206) 325-7442
www.rovers-seattle.com

SALISBURY HOUSE
750 16th Avenue E
Seattle, WA 98112
(206) 328-8682
www.salisburyhouse.com

SALMON HOUSE ON THE HILL
2229 Folkestone Way
West Vancouver, BC V7S 2Y6
Canada
(604) 926-3212
www.salmonhouse.com

SEL GRIS
1852 SE Hawthorne Boulevard
Portland, OR 97214
(503) 517-7770
www.selgris.net

SITKA & SPRUCE
2238 Eastlake Avenue E
Seattle, WA 98102
(206) 324-0662
www.sitkaandspruce.com

SOL DUC HOT SPRINGS
PO Box 2169
Port Angeles, WA 98362
(866) 476-5382
(360) 327-3583
www.visitsolduc.com

SOOKE HARBOUR HOUSE
1528 Whiffen Spit
Sooke, BC V0S 1N0
(250) 642-3421
www.sookeharbourhouse.com

STEPHANIE INN
PO Box 219
2740 S Pacific Street
Cannon Beach, OR 97110
(800) 633-3466
(503) 436-2221
www.stephanie-inn.com

STONEHEDGE GARDENS
3405 Cascade Drive
Hood River, OR 97031
(541) 386-3940

THE SUTTON PLACE HOTEL
845 Burrard Street
Vancouver, BC V6Z 2K6
Canada
(604) 682-5511
www.vancouver.suttonplace.com

SYLVIA BEACH HOTEL
267 NW Cliff Street
Newport, OR 97365
(541) 265-5428
www.sylviabeachhotel.com

TILTH
1411 N 45th Street
Seattle, WA 98103
(206) 633-0801
www.tilthrestaurant.com

TOKELAND HOTEL & RESTAURANT
100 Hotel Road
Tokeland, WA 98590
(360) 267-7006
www.tokelandhotel.com

TURTLEBACK FARM INN
1981 Crow Valley Road
Eastsound, WA 98245
(360) 376-4914
www.turtlebackinn.com

VIJ'S
1480 11th Avenue W
Vancouver, BC V6H 1L1
(604) 736-6664
www.vijs.ca

WEST
2881 Granville Street
Vancouver, BC VH 3J4
(604) 738-8938
www.westrestaurant.com

WHARFSIDE BED & BREAKFAST
Slip 13, Port of Friday Harbor Marina,
Box 1212
Friday Harbor, WA 98250
(360) 378-5661
www.slowseason.com

THE WHITE SWAN GUEST HOUSE
15872 Moore Road
Mt. Vernon, WA 98273
(360) 445-6805
www.thewhiteswan.com

WILD GINGER
1401 3rd Avenue
Seattle, WA 98101
(206) 623-4450
www.wildginger.net

WILDWOOD
1221 NW 21st Avenue
Portland, OR 97209
(503) 248-9663
www.wildwoodrestaurant.com

index

acknowledgments

THANKS TO my intrepid crew of recipe testers, Matthew Amster-Burton, Rina Jordan, Peabody Rudd, Jess Thomson, Eric & Dawn Wright, and Matt & Danika Wright for their quick response and excellent feedback that helped make these recipes even better. A special thanks to Claire Bloomberg, who not only tested the recipes, but also performed amazing feats of food styling to help get the artwork done on time. To my team at Sasquatch, you made working on this project a breeze. Finally, I owe a debt of gratitude to my husband, Cameron, and daughter, Cole, for patiently putting up with my whirlwind schedule and occasional work sessions during our summer vacation.

—*LF*

MANY THANKS TO our local chefs, winemakers, growers, and producers for making the Northwest one of the most delicious regions in the world. The authors also gratefully acknowledge the recipe-testing help they received from Susan Fowler Volland, Gwendolyn Hayes, and Tim and Katherine Kehrli. Thanks from Cynthia to Bob for his never-ending willingness to be on the tasting end of the tests; thanks from Lori to Tony for his vision and inspiration.

—*CN & LM*

about the authors

LARA FERRONI is a former tech geek turned food geek who spends her days exploring the food culture of the Northwest. As a food writer and photographer, she might be spotted learning to make kimchi in the back rooms of a local church, chatting with local vendors at farmers markets, foraging for wild berries, or snapping away in the kitchens at Rover's. She regularly contributes to Epicurious.com, *Portland Monthly Magazine*, *edibleSEATTLE*, and *Seattle* magazine. You can find more of her tasty photos and recipes on her blog, Cook & Eat (www.cookandeat.com).

LORI MCKEAN, author of *Pacific Northwest Flavors*, is a former chef and cooking teacher who studied at the Ballymaloe Cookery School in Ireland. She has served as food editor for *Northwest Palate* magazine and contributing editor to *Regions Northwest*. Her articles on food and wine have appeared in *Bon Appétit*, *Better Homes & Gardens*, and *The Wine Enthusiast*, among others.

CYNTHIA C. NIMS is the food editor of *Seattle* magazine, local editor of the Zagat restaurant survey, and a freelance food and travel writer. She is the author of *The Best Places Northwest Desserts Cookbook* and many others, including *The Northwest Best Places Cookbook, Volume 2*; *Crab*; and *Stone Fruit*.